The English Village Green

D1360702

The English Village Green

Brian Bailey

Robert Hale · London

© Brian Bailey 1985
First published in Great Britain 1985

British Library Cataloguing in Publication Data

Bailey, Brian
The English village green
1. Villages—England
I. Title
942′.009′734   DA667
ISBN 0-7090-2339-1

Robert Hale Limited
Clerkenwell House
Clerkenwell Green
London EC1

Designed by Geoffrey Wadsley
Photoset and printed in Great Britain
by BAS Printers Ltd., Over Wallop, Hampshire
Bound by WBC Bookbinders Ltd.

Contents

List of Illustrations

Black and white plates

Colour plates

Acknowledgements

The copyright photographs in this book have been supplied by the following. The Author: pp. 20–1, 28, 38, 42, 48, 69 (below), 78, 80, 83, 87 (above), 91, 93–4, 98–100, 102, 104–5, 107–8, 110, 116–117, 124–6, 128, 178, 180, 183, 194, 196–201, 205–6. Alan Kirk: 15, 29, 39, 47, 121 (above), 122, 132–3, 135, 139 (above), 143–4, 146–8, 150–2, 154–5, 160, 163 (below), 166, 168–9, 176–7, 204, 210. Van Phillips: 17, 74. Kenneth Scowen: 18, 35 (below), 41, 44, 49, 54, 57–8, 59–60, 64, 72–3, 85, 88, 115, 130, 184, 186. Geoffrey N. Wright: 26, 139 (below), 156. Rita Bailey: 35 (above), 36, 70, 87 (below), 173, 191. The Mansell Collection: 51 (above). Mary Evans Picture Library: 51 (below). Roy J. Westlake: 69 (above), 174. AA Photolibrary: 121 (below). Derek G. Widdicombe: 140, 163 (above), 164, 192 (above). Derek G. Widdicombe/Frieda Stanbury: 192 (below).

Foreword

The village green is a part of the consciousness of those of us brought up in or near the English countryside. That view is parochial; of course there are village greens everywhere but for most of us they are part of growing up; they belong to our childhood and youth; and to that extent, especially in the days before car ownership became general, the experience was local: and that means as different in detail as rural England can be.

Mr Bailey's history – how surprising that he should be the first historian of such an attractive subject – is at times salutary. He calls up the days when the village green could be the scene of the local baron's savage 'justice'. For those of today, though, William Blake saw it with his characteristic crystalline simplicity in 'Songs of Innocence'.

> The skylark and thrush,
> The birds of the bush,
> Sing louder around
> To the bells' cheerful sound,
> While our sports shall be seen
> On the Echoing Green.
>
> Old John, with white hair,
> Does laugh away care,
> Sitting under the oak,
> Among the old folk.
> They laugh at our play
> And soon they all say:
> 'Such, such were the joys
> When we all, girls and boys,
> In our youth time were seen
> On the Echoing Green.'

Certainly in the first quarter of this century there were villagers to whom the green was the more precious for the fact that their forebears had fought for it against the would-be enclosers. Essentially, though, it is a place for pleasure; but also, in its way, the hub of the village. The village green of memory is a composite picture

11

from many. Around it is set the church, the vicarage, the village pub, the general shop (also the post office) and the village hall. At its centre is the cricket pitch, fenced off – after much bitter argument with non-cricketing parish councillors – to protect it against cattle, vehicles and small boys with minds to excavation.

It is the place for the young and the old. For this writer, too, a corner of one special and particular Hampshire village green was the scene of his first courtship and his first serious kiss. Perhaps that is why the sight of a village green is still so piquantly nostalgic.

John Arlott

—— I ——
Origins and Distribution

It is an extraordinary thing that, among all the fine essays from the acknowledged masters of that once most popular of literary forms, there is not one about village greens. I have searched diligently in Steele and Addison, Hazlitt and Leigh Hunt, Chesterton and Belloc, E. V. Lucas and Robert Lynd, A. A. Milne and J. B. Priestley, to find some illuminating reflection on this most obvious of English subjects, but without success. Not even Charles Lamb, who loved Hertfordshire (the king of counties when it comes to village greens), seems to have contrived a piece on the triangular patch of grass at so many village centres. No doubt, the minute this book is published, some erudite reader will point out a perfectly well-known essay by someone that I have carelessly missed, but before he or she does so, I offer an extended essay myself on a most deserving feature of the English scene.

The English village green is a little patch of grassland that still strikes a chord in the hearts of most native men and women two hundred years after the Industrial Revolution changed the majority of us to urban dwellers. It represents rural peace and quiet, as well as a community spirit that does not obtain in towns, and sets up in most of us a yearning for that fondly imagined country paradise, lost by the growth of imperialism and capitalism which have made England an over-populated country of noisy and dirty towns and cities where the mass of men, as Thoreau put it, lead lives of quiet desperation.

That often quite small and apparently insignificant bit of green land at the village centre exercises a curious magic to befuddle the thoughts of industrial man, but he does not usually think of the village green as one of the greatest mysteries of rural history and one of the biggest anachronisms of twentieth-century life in western Europe. Yet the origin of the village green remains a riddle, its survival a cause for wonder, and its status a contradiction of all our most deeply cherished beliefs.

Conservative Englishmen who believe that Communism is the most evil idea ever perpetrated by the perverse minds of wicked men can be seen daily walking their dogs over communal village greens where for centuries, as Bernard Shaw might have put it, their forbears watered their livestock at the communal horse-pond, danced their children round the communal maypole, punished their felons in the communal stocks and drew their water from the communal pump.

So when did village greens first appear, and what was their purpose? The most commonly held view today seems to be that they originally had a defensive function, but there is plenty of room for doubt about that, and I, for one, do not believe it. It seems probable, if not certain, that the village green was introduced into Britain by the Angles, Saxons, Jutes and Frisians who settled here from the fifth century onwards, after invading a vulnerable island left to fend for itself by the departing Roman legions. The Roman concept of social organization did not include villages, and the pre-Roman settlements of which we have evidence do not appear to have included a central piece of land reserved for common use. The ancient Britons gathered in communities for self-defence against marauding wolves and hostile tribes, but not with any clearly formulated communal planning. They had a sense of safety in numbers, but not of planning strategy. They erected their huts and shelters within defensive banks and ditches or wooden pallisades, and cleared the forest round these enclosures for agricultural development. Sometimes the settlements were only temporary, and they were generally on the uplands of western England rather than on the intractable clay soil of the eastern lowlands.

East Witton, North Yorkshire. The close formation of houses round this long green has prompted the idea that it once had a defensive function.

The Roman occupation was a period in which the ideas of private property and class distinction were promoted, but in northern Europe at this time the barbarian tribes held and administered their land on a communal basis, and it is from this region that the Angles and Saxons began to make inroads into Britain when the obstacle of the Roman military machine had been removed.

Villages of Anglo-Saxon foundation were primarily in the south and east, where the settlers' superior ploughs could cope with the heavy soil, and it is chiefly in these lowland regions of England that the village green is still to be found. But this fact seems to contradict the view that village greens originated for defensive purposes. For it is not in the southern lowlands that we find the classic examples of apparently defensive village planning, but in the north, where they were influenced not so much by the Anglo-Saxon settlement of the fifth century as by the Danish and Norse ones of a few centuries later. Nevertheless, evidence suggests that early Anglo-Saxon villages did usually consist of huts arranged round an empty open area, so maybe the warlike Scandinavian settlers were simply more sophisticated in their awareness of defensive strategy. It is difficult at first to imagine why else lowland villages should have been arranged round a piece of bare ground, but of course the path of human knowledge is littered with discarded assumptions we have tried to justify through ignorance, and when you see classic examples of what seem like defensively planned villages in northern England, such as Milburn in Cumbria and East Witton in North Yorkshire, it is very hard to believe that the tiny triangular or irregularly shaped greens of the south were ever conceived with defence in mind.

Visible reinforcement of the argument in favour of defensive function may seem clear at Milburn and East Witton and several other northern villages where centuries of village encroachment and evolution have not blotted out the features these places were apparently born with.

Milburn is a compact nucleated village arranged tightly round a broad rectangular green. Its rendered and limewashed cottages and farm buildings stand in

close formation all round it like the circles of covered wagons so familiar to us in Hollywood epics about the Wild West, although it is worth remarking that here the dwellings face inward, to the green, and not outward to the attacking forces. (How much more sensible it would seem, if the houses were supposed to be defending the village green, to have them facing outwards, like those at Northaw in Hertford-shire, where the back gardens of the houses run down to a triangular green. Yet this layout is rare.) Access is available to Milburn's green only at the four corners of the rectangle. The two roads at the eastern side lead nowhere, and so, with no through traffic, Milburn enjoys an unusual quietness at its centre today.

In East Witton's case, the green is of slightly less regular shape but may be de-scribed as a rough oblong. The houses huddle together along both sides, and roads lead in from both ends, though the main road bypasses the green. Both here and at Milburn, the church stands outside the village nucleus.

The argument for defensive origins is that these villages were planned in this way so that in times of danger the villagers could bring their livestock onto the central green and block the access points against their enemies. These might be cattle-raiders in early times or Scottish barbarians during the medieval border troubles. The theory sounds reasonable at first sight, especially when you consider that African tribesmen do precisely this today, forming a central compound with their huts to protect their livestock from lions and other predators. But the idea must be called into serious question on several counts.

First and foremost, if this was such a brilliant idea, why were not *all* villages planned this way? For all villages in the same region were vulnerable to the same attacks, and even though all villages were not founded at the same time, the great variations in village plans are not entirely accounted for by differences in age. Moreover, the idea that such defensive villages were a strategic response to the trou-bled Scottish border region begs the question why there are hardly any green villages of any sort at all in the equally turbulent Welsh Marches.

Secondly, if 'green' villages were planned for defence very early in their lifetimes, why were not those such as Milburn and East Witton built beside the streams which not only provided their essential water supply but would have constituted an addi-tional defensive barrier?

Furthermore, the villages in the south of England were preoccupied with arable rather than pastoral farming, so did not need central reservations for large herds of livestock, though their greens are sometimes just as large as those in the north. Besides, the 'ing' name ending, from the Old English *ingas*, is usually reckoned to distinguish many of the earliest Anglo-Saxon settlements, yet in a county such as Essex, for instance, which has a large number of 'ing' names and a large number

Kew Green, London. The extensive green of this former village is now an urban open area of the metropolis south of the Thames.

Paddington Green, London. The old village green is a remarkable survival, only a stone's throw from the capital city's West End.

Finchingfield, Essex. One of the best known and most popular of England's village greens.

of village greens, the two features do not coincide except in a small number of cases such as the Rodings and Finchingfield.

We must also bear in mind the fragility of Anglo-Saxon peasant houses, which were usually of the type called in Germany *Grubenhäuser*. They consisted of shallow pits roofed over with flimsy thatched structures that came down to the ground on two sides like a tent, and were closed with end walls of timber, one of which had the doorway in it. It would be ludicrous to suppose that these hovels could be defended against armed attack, and there is no reason to assume that Anglo-Saxons were more stupid than Celts and Romans before them or the Normans after them, all of whom knew that the best way to defend yourself against an aggressor was to surround yourself with a ditch, a pallisade or a high wall.

Then again, how much advance warning could isolated villages have had of impending raids which would give the inhabitants time to go out and round up all their livestock from the widely scattered pastures, drive the animals into the village centre, and close up all the gaps before the raiders turned up? I think we had better start again.

Some may see the final nail in the defensive theory's coffin being hammered in when we ask the obvious question – why are the churches at Milburn and East Witton, and so many other villages, outside the village centres? If they were Christian communities early in the growth of the villages, you would expect the church to be at the centre, as it is in the majority of English villages. In the example of East Witton, it is believed by some that the original settlement *was* centred on the ancient church and that it was only when the abbot of Jervaulx Abbey became lord of the manor that the new village began to develop around a central green in the fourteenth century, to accommodate the fair and market the abbot had founded. If this is the case, then many greens were perhaps a later development than we have hitherto supposed, and were no part of the early settlers' strategy.

Although this idea may possibly be true in certain cases, I do not think we can be sure that the siting of a green away from the church proves generally that the original centre was round the church and that the green came later, as several writers assume. I cannot see that this conclusion follows logically from the evidence, except to bigoted Christians, and indeed, I would have thought the exact opposite could be argued just as convincingly. Why could not the church be built outside the green area of the village so as not to encroach upon the community centre? After all, as Lord Melbourne said: 'Things have come to a pretty pass when religion is allowed to invade the sphere of private life.' How much more true might this have been to practical and only recently heathen Anglo-Saxons scarcely converted to Christianity?

Village wells and pumps
Above: Farmington, Gloucestershire. The gabled well-housing was presented to the village by the people of Farmington, Connecticut, in 1898.

Left: Dufton, Cumbria. This maroon-painted pump is the purple patch in a Pennine village of green grass and trees and dark northern stone.

Right: Preston, Hertfordshire. Well-head winding gear protected by a heptagonal housing with roof of slate.

Right: Aldworth, Berkshire. This elaborate structure takes up practically all of what is left of the former village green.

In northern Europe, especially in Germany, where nucleated villages known as *Angerdörfen* are grouped round long rectangular or oval greens just like those at Milburn and East Witton, it has been shown that the village pattern was related to the open field system of farming. When early communities cleared forests to create land on which they could grow their crops as well as land on which to graze their animals, they sited their villages between the two types for easy access to both. And in parts of Scandinavia, the system known as *solskifte* was introduced in the Middle Ages, whereby villages were re-planned with the houses arranged clockwise round an empty area, following the course of the sun, and in the same order as the strips in the open fields. This was probably done to facilitate feudal controls and assessments, and it seems quite probable that English villages like East Witton and Milburn, where Scandinavian influence was strong, were also reorganized on this system, establishing new village centres apart from their churches. The greens would have been land held in common, where livestock could be grazed in winter and, perhaps more importantly, protected at night from wolves, which were once common in Britain. The name 'Ulpha' meaning wolf, occurs frequently in northern England, where the classic 'defensive' villages are to be found, and wolves ravaged the flocks of sheep until the last one was reputedly killed in the Cartmel district in the sixteenth century.

One possibility which has not been proposed, as far as I know, is that small greens were conceived as central areas reserved for the protection of the common water supply and to give access to it. It is easy for us in these days of piped water to every home to overlook how the absolutely overriding consideration in the establishment of any village or hamlet was the availability of water. When a well was dug, with great labour, to supply all the villagers with their water, it must have been regarded with a protective reverence that we find hard to imagine today. In areas of water scarcity, such as the Chiltern Hills, where rainwater soaks quickly through the chalk rock, even village ponds are often artificial, having been dug and lined with clay bonded with straw to retain the water. How precious these primitive reservoirs were is attested to by the sentimental survival of so many village pumps, which no longer have any practical use, and by the survival of ritual worship of wells in places like the Peak District of Derbyshire. And of course they are usually to be found on village greens, often still carefully protected from vandals and pollution. They stand like symbols of village continuity, and it might be that many greens were regarded as precincts sacred to the community's source of life. It would hardly be surprising if some defensive measures were taken to protect the village pump or well just as much as livestock. An obvious way for an enemy to attack a community would have been to pollute its water supply. On the uplands of western Britain, of course, water was not so scarce, which is why the earliest inhabitants settled there.

We might usefully enquire at this point why it is that so many village greens, particularly in the south of England, are triangular. Their incidence is far too great to be merely accidental, and there must have been good reasons, surely, why they were laid out in this way. Not that we can be absolutely sure that they were originally this shape. It is possible that the villages began haphazardly but had this nucleated plan imposed on them later. Apart from the obvious fact (if we cling to the defensive theory) that it would be easier to defend entrances at three points than at four, what practical purpose could be served by having a three-cornered village centre?

First of all, as there are so many triangular greens, it might seem obvious that this shape was ordained by authority at some point, even if it became merely traditional later on. So common a plan could hardly have evolved by chance over such a wide area with scattered settlers – some of them probably with poor communications – all hitting on the same idea. If the triangular plan was imposed in local areas, it must have been by the lords of manors and was thus clearly related to the open field system of farming like the *solskifte* system in Denmark and Sweden.

The customary, though not universal, number of open fields in feudal England, was three. Two were cultivated in strips and one was left fallow each year, in rotation, and the peasants not only worked their own strips but were obliged to tend their lord's land as well as serve his military needs. Now it is improbable that the lord's bailiff organized his labour force by a rota system that named Tom, Dick or Harry for duty on a certain day. Much more likely that simple administration was afforded by a three-sided layout matching the open fields surrounding the village, so that the lord of the manor and his agents (in language made familiar to us by the place-name experts) could call upon 'the dwellers by the west field' and so on. This, or something like it, seems a much more likely explanation of village planning than any defensive or protective function.

But all the elaborate theories we can dream up do not entirely rule out the possibility that the shapes of greens were almost accidental, and arranged according to communications with neighbouring settlements. If a village lay on a road between two neighbours in line, say along the course of a river, the chances are that it would develop as a linear or 'street' village. If its centre was at the junction of *three* roads, it would have a triangular open space; if *four*, it would be likely to grow in importance more rapidly and develop a market square.

Against this 'accidental' approach, however, we can find some powerful additional evidence. For instance, quite a number of villages have more than one green. Where we find two pieces of irregularly shaped green close together, separated by

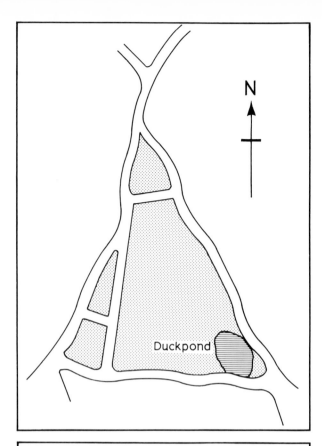

Sketch plans (not to scale) of three distinctive types of village green:

Left: **Writtle, Essex**
A simple triangular green which has been split up by roadways. In the south-east corner is the duckpond. The parish church is a short distance away from the green on the south side.

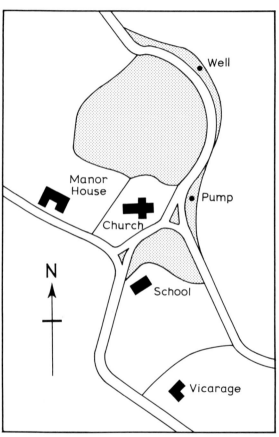

Above: **Hellidon, Northants**
A much more complicated layout where the original green has been fragmented by road-making and building encroachment. The two greens and the roadside verges were undoubtedly all one green once.

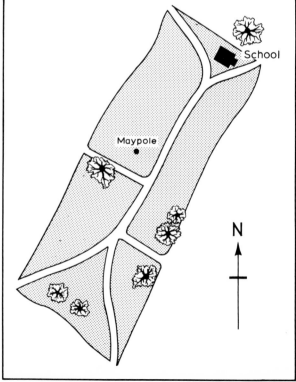

Left: **Milburn, Cumbria**
A rectangular green with access points at the four corners. There are trees on and around the green, which is completely and closely surrounded by cottages and farm buildings. A permanent maypole stands on the green and the village school is on the northern triangle. The church is outside this strictly planned nucleus.

a road and a few houses, we can generally assume that they were originally parts of one larger green on which encroachment has occurred over the centuries. But where there are two distinct triangular greens some distance apart, it is more likely that the village was split up between two medieval manors, each with its own green. A few villages have, or once had, several greens, and it may be that in some such cases each green belonged to a different manor. It was, after all, the lord of the manor who obtained licence to hold fairs and markets, and he would have to have an open space on his own manorial lands for such events, quite apart from the older questions of feudal administration.

Some interesting reinforcement of the geographical distinctions of planned greens is provided by the study of deserted medieval villages. Often of Anglo-Saxon foundation and abandoned during the Middle Ages for reasons of climate, pestilence or capitalist enclosure, depopulated villages are often shown by excavation or aerial photography to have had greens or open spaces at their centres. Thus the lost village of Walworth in County Durham had a fairly large square green at its centre with the houses grouped closely round it, exactly like the surviving green villages in the county today. But the village of Clopton in Cambridgeshire, destroyed in order to create pasture for sheep, had a smaller triangular green in the fork of a road junction, typical of the greens of southern England.

It seems, on balance, that village greens were probably made at different times and for different reasons, and the only thing we can say with reasonable confidence about their origins is that they were held in common by the villagers. The simplest view we can take of village greens, and undoubtedly the most accurate generalization we can make on the subject, is that they originated as central open spaces or precincts for farming communities where villagers could not only gather their livestock for safety at night but congregate to discuss their farming programme, celebrate their festivals and meet the lord of the manor when the latter required it. The modern equivalent is the village hall. Local needs dictated some differences in size and layout, but the function of all greens was basically the same – an open space where common as opposed to individual activities were practised.

This brings us to the distinction between a village green and a 'common', and here again we run into some difficulties of definition. The largest areas of common land are on the western and northern uplands of Britain where the familiar pattern of settlement is of scattered farmsteads rather than nucleated villages. So-called 'common' land is now all privately owned, but originally it was held in common, and the present-day owners of common land have to recognize very ancient surface rights which are still in force and jealously guarded, in particular the rights of local people – known as commoners – to graze their animals on it and gather wood for

Hutton-le-Hole, North Yorkshire. When is a green not a green? When it's a common! Sheep graze freely among the cottages scattered about on this common land on the North York Moors.

fuel. The freedom of all of us to wander over common land at will is not so much a right as a time-honoured custom. The village green may also be subject to rights of common grazing, but at any rate the simple distinction between a common and a village green nowadays is that the common is privately owned and the green is the common property of the village, as it has remained for something like fifteen hundred years.

Another problem of definition concerns size. How small does a patch of grass at the centre of a village have to be in order to be disqualified as a village green? Clearly a green barely large enough for half a dozen villagers to stand on can hardly be called communal, but there are many greens supporting a war memorial or a tree with a seat under it which are the remnants of once-larger greens. Thus Dorset, which is officially credited with only two village greens in the returns submitted to the Royal Commission on Common Land after the Second World War, has some like the tiny triangular wayside green at Evershot, which would increase the numbers considerably. Similarly, a tiny wayside green with a war memorial on it, such as that at Ogbourne St Andrew in Wiltshire, must be considered a green now, even if it was only roadside waste at one time, because the memorial invests it with a communal meaning and gives the villagers a common interest in its upkeep. Many small pieces of roadside waste, turned to advantage in this or other ways, are nowadays much better looked after than many a larger area which is by both law and custom a proper village green at the ancient centre of a settlement.

In the days of open-field farming, when a village grew, it had either to encroach outwards onto valuable farmland or inwards onto the communal central area. Thus many greens disappeared altogether. Some 'green' villages may have become 'street' villages in this way.

In upland settlements where the main preoccupation was pastoral farming, owners of large flocks of sheep would not have had much use for a small village green which could support only a few sheep, goats and geese, and in any case, vast tracts of grassland on hills and moors which were no good for cultivation were available as grazing land. The extreme scarcity of greens in Wales and Cornwall is clear enough evidence that green villages were not a Celtic speciality. But in the lowlands of the south and east, where the importance of fertile soil to the Anglo-Saxon settlers is equally clear, forests had been cleared specifically for cultivation of the soil which provided their food and gave them employment. Turning such land over to pasture was to become a source of fierce and long-fought disputes. In the villages of these areas, the communal green was a valuable and convenient patch of grassland for the smaller numbers of animals the villagers owned.

Hence we find a very large concentration of village greens in the south Midlands

Contrasts in size and shape

Left: Stretton-on-Dunsmore, Warwickshire. A triangular Midland green just big enough for a signpost and a seat round the tree.

Right: Ackworth, West Yorkshire. A well cared-for green of modest size with several trees and seats as well as the old village cross.

Right: West Auckland, Durham. One of the characteristically large greens in this county.

and the Home Counties. Roughly ten per cent of English villages have greens, but nearly a third of them occur in seven counties in and around London – Bedfordshire, Berkshire, Buckinghamshire, Essex, Hertfordshire, Middlesex and Surrey. Before the local government reorganization of the seventies, Hertfordshire came out easily on top, with well over a hundred greens. Its nearest rival in the south was Surrey. But since 1974 those counties' greens have been outnumbered by those of the new county of Cumbria, which comprises Cumberland, Westmorland and former parts of Lancashire and North Yorkshire. Cumbria apart, however, we shall find the vast majority of village greens down the eastern half of England, in those areas where stone villages, which are characteristic of the western uplands, do not occur.

One part of eastern England where village greens are notably absent is the fen country. Nearly two thousand square miles of land under shallow sea-water were totally uninhabited until reclamation of the land, begun on a small scale by the Romans, was carried out in earnest in the seventeenth century by the Dutch engineer Cornelius Vermuyden. The reclaimed soil was among the most fertile in Britain and much too valuable to be given up to communal leisure-use, which was the only real purpose village greens had by that time.

This emphasizes the fact that village greens were made in response to particular needs at particular times, and when we come across one or two modern estate villages with greens at their centres, we may attribute them to a strong rural tradition in England that demands imitation. We all like to see an attractive green, and green villages have appeared most frequently among the 'best-kept' villages of England. Caution about what are and what are not village greens inclines me to point out, also, that small seaside resorts, often having areas of grassland near the sea-front and looking a bit like village greens, are usually quite modern bits of amenity planning and will thus usually be ignored here.

In the chapters which follow, readers will find that the greens I mention do not conform very closely to the lists of village greens submitted to the Royal Commission on Common Land set up in 1955 and published in *The Common Lands of England and Wales* by two members of the Commission, W. G. Hoskins and L. Dudley Stamp. The reasons for this are various. In the first place, I make no attempt in this book to mention all the village greens in England, so many are listed there which will not be found here. Secondly, I have come across many greens in my travels which were not included in the official returns to the Commission as either greens or commons. It may be that the legal status of such greens is such that the county authorities responsible for those returns were right to omit them, but I suspect that quite a number of true village greens were left out which ought to have been included. At any rate, I have not allowed the absence of a green from those returns to deter me from including here any green that *looks* like a village green, has all the charac-teristics of a village green and is believed by everyone to *be* a village green. To give a mere couple of examples of seeming incompleteness, neither the green at Aldbury, Hertfordshire, nor that at Meriden, West Midlands, was apparently mentioned to the Royal Commission. These are two of the best-known village greens in England.

Not least among the attractions of village greens in general are the delightful names they have often given to the settlements around them, conjuring up instant visions of the charm of rural England, tucked away peacefully along narrow lanes where the noise and rush and squalor of modern Britain have so far thankfully failed to penetrate. The more lyrical and curious of England's green village names are mostly confined to the south, away from the harsh and gritty northern accents inherited from the Vikings and Danes.

The names of little rural greens are not necessarily as old as the greens themselves, and indeed, many of the names that we think most 'quaint' may be relatively recent appellations. Foxhunt Green in East Sussex. for instance, is clearly a fairly modern name, since fox-hunting did not begin as an organized sport until the early eighteenth century.

A 'green' name is no guarantee, moreover, that there is a village green there today. It may have been built over long ago or turned into a paved square as a more up-to-date village centre, but the place will not have changed its name on that account. In most cases, however, the green is happily still there, and from Partridge Green in Sussex and Beggarman's Green in Hertfordshire to Fiddlers Green in Hampshire and Pixey Green in Suffolk, the enticing names beckon us with hints of rural serenity and seclusion. These little patches of grass are emeralds set in the rings worn on England's right hand.

— II —

The Use of Village Greens

Whatever the original purpose of village greens may have been, there is much more certainty about the uses to which they have been put over the centuries. Although each green is different in size, shape and history, some generalizations are perhaps permissible in postulating the social history of a typical village green from Domesday to 1984, if you will pardon that somewhat ominous choice of chronology.

Let us give our hypothetical green a triangular shape and place it somewhere in the middle of England, where the economy at Domesday is based on growing wheat, oats and barley. We will assume an area of rough grass of three or four acres, with a pond at one corner, near the village church, which is a low timber building. There is an oak tree near the middle of the green and a well to one side, dug generations ago, from which the village draws its entire water supply. One old man can remember being told by his grandfather how all water, for washing, drinking and watering the animals, had to be fetched in his day from a stream which was fed from a natural spring half a mile away. The well has brought to the village all mod cons.

The 'houses' round the three sides of the green are primitive wattle-and-daub huts of one room, roofed with thick blankets of straw from the harvest and frequently renewed. Straw is also scattered on the floors of bare earth. The peasants who live in them spend most of their lives cultivating the three open fields round the village and performing various services for the lord of the manor, including the cultivation of his own private land, which is more than all the villagers own between them. They maintain a plough team of eight oxen. Most of them are in theory free men, but they are always subject to their lord's demands. There is a long tradition of complete loyalty to one's lord, but that does not mean that the peasants like or respect him, for they are not fools. They see him as a necessary evil – a despot upon whom their livelihoods are utterly dependent.

They do not see the lord of the manor often, for although there is a manor house outside the village, built of stone which the village men had to quarry, the lord does not live in it. He owns a small castle some distance away, for he has authority from the king over a vast area of land and only visits the village during his progresses through his various manors to supervise his affairs and make sure that his bailiff, who lives in the manor house, is protecting his lord's interests.

There is no road across the green, but there are well-trodden paths in the rough grass. A few geese and one or two sheep graze it, and children and dogs run about on it. The peasants also have some pigs, but they are kept either in a wood beyond the open fields or in whichever field is left fallow each year, for the three fields are cultivated in rotation by communal agreement, and the peasants gather together on the green each winter to agree on the farming programme for the coming spring. It is only in the last two hundred years or so, since King Alfred's time, that peasants have been allowed to own anything themselves – before then everything belonged to the lord of the manor, and most of it still does.

When the ploughing and sowing have been done, the peasants pay lip-service in the church to the Christian prayers for good crops, but they do not really under-stand this – it is all in Latin – and they have their own pagan ceremonies on the green which have been performed by their ancestors from time immemorial.

When the lord of the manor visits the village, they do not understand him either, for he speaks French, and the bailiff acts as interpreter. One of the lord's purposes in coming is to dispense justice, and he will usually hold court in a room of the manor house, but when the weather is fine, he may do so on the green. All the villagers and the lord's serfs are required to be present, for the purpose of punishment is deterrence, and it will be meted out on the spot. Women and children watch in silence as the menfolk take part in the proceedings, though the women themselves are often the subject of the action. One man's daughter is visibly pregnant, though unmarried, and a fine is due to the lord. The child, as a bastard, will be deemed a free man, and the lord will therefore suffer a financial loss, whereas if the girl were married, the child would be his property. The lord demands twelve pence.

The bailiff tells the lord that one of the peasants stole another man's loaf of bread. The felon stands before the lord, trembling with fear while he awaits the sentence. The villagers look on apprehensively. The lord might have him hanged forthwith from the oak tree or have his eyes put out. The bailiff tells the lord that the man does his work well and stole the bread because he has a larger family than most (which is to the lord's advantage), and last season's poor harvest did not provide for his needs. The lord decides to be merciful and orders merely that the man's right hand be cut off. Two servants bring the man to a wooden block and hold him with his arm laid across it; another man performs the punishment with one great blow from a wood-chopper. The shriek of the victim sets the dogs barking as his spurting blood soaks into the grass and leaves a trail across the green as he staggers half conscious to the further agony of having the bleeding stump cauterised. He will not be able to work so well in future. His children will have to make up for his deficiency. The severed hand is burnt at once so as not to attract unwanted scavengers to the green.

Life goes on in much the same way for two centuries, with only minimal changes. Houses fall down and have to be rebuilt, or are burnt down accidentally in winter through having fires too big. There is a little more livestock on the green as peasants prosper and more of them become free men with the right to own a little property. Every few years the pond and the well both dry up in long, hot summers, and water has to be carried from the spring. The new young lord of the manor speaks English when he comes to the village. He is very prosperous, as a result of his service to the king, and comes with an entourage of his knights and squires, family and servants, to stay in the manor house for a month or two, bringing his best bed and linen, his food and wine, tapestries to hang on the walls, his dogs and horses, falcons, weapons and jewels.

No sooner have the villagers got over the mild excitement of this event than cartloads of stone begin to be brought into the village, dragged by horses and oxen from a quarry many miles away. The carts are trundled with great difficulty over the bumpy green, and the stone is unloaded on the grass in front of the church. Some of the men are called to help. Gradually the rumour gets round that the lord of the manor is going to pull down the wooden church and rebuild it in stone, with a steeple. There are no masons among the villagers and only one carpenter, so many strangers start to appear in the village, and new huts are built to accommodate them. Some of the huts are put up on the green itself, for the difficulty of hauling the carts of stone over the grass has led to a rough track being cut through it from the road outside the village, and the area between this track and the church is the obvious place for the builders to settle themselves and their equipment. There is some muttering of discontent among the villagers, for there is less room for their sheep, goats and geese now, but it is more than their lives are worth to make open complaints.

Meanwhile, the new church gradually rises from its foundations, causing wonder among the local people, for only one or two of them have ever been to the big town where the first church of stone in the district was completed a few years earlier.

Hartley Wintney,
Hampshire. Cricketers
Green, with the inn of that
name beside it, is one of
several in this large
village.

Swan Green, Hampshire.
Autumn on this delightful
New Forest green near
Lyndhurst.

dbourne, Wiltshire. An
iglo-Saxon village green
hich has remained much
e same for centuries
hile the church and
uses round it have
anged relatively often.

The old men wag their heads, as old men will, and predict that the steeple will fall down as soon as the March winds blow. When the church is finished, after many years of labour, the houses that were built for the craftsmen and labourers remain, as they are now taken for granted, and everyone has forgotten that the area they stand on rightly belongs to the village green. Dwellings there from now on are used by the village's increasing population.

Thus far, the story of this green has been largely speculative, but from this point it is possible to feel a little more secure in our hypothesis and to provide examples of the same sort of things happening elsewhere. For instance, the men of the village practise archery on the green, with longbows cut from the yew trees in the church-yard. They wrestle and take other forms of exercise, too, for all of them are required to be soldiers when the need arises. One day a messenger comes from the lord of the manor and summons all the people to the green to hear his news. The king has decreed that training in archery will henceforth be compulsory for every able-bodied man on Sundays.

During the Middle Ages, the soldiers whom English kings took to their foreign wars were trained on the village greens of England. The practice of archery was encouraged by statute from the reign of Edward III, and men like Henry V's 'band of brothers' who, numbering but nine thousand, defeated a French army of twenty thousand at Agincourt on St Crispin's Day in 1415 gained their superior skills at the butts on village greens. Right up to the Tudor period, every fit Englishman was required to be proficient in the use of the longbow in readiness for conscription in the national service. Hugh Latimer, the Leicestershire lad who became Bishop of Worcester under Henry VIII and was burnt at the stake by Mary I, described how his father had taught him, when he was a boy, 'how to draw, how to lay my body in my bow, and not to draw with strength of arm as other nations do, but with strength of body. I had my bows bought me according to my age and strength; as I increased in them, so my bows were made bigger and bigger, for men shall never shoot well unless they be brought up in it.' Thus the village greens of England were training grounds for the finest infantry in medieval Europe.

Meanwhile, however, soldiers returning from abroad and merchants trading with foreign countries have brought home rumours of a terrible calamity in the Far East, and slowly the story filters through to the villagers of our hypothetical community, but the news has been so slow in reaching them, and the spread of the pestilence so fast, that almost before they have heard the rumour many of them are struck down by the disease, in the summer of 1349. The symptoms are great boils, some-times as big as an apple, in the groin or armpits, or alternatively a high fever and spitting of blood. The villagers – men, women and children – go down like ninepins,

Aldbourne, Wiltshire. The green was undoubtedly here before the Norman church was built, and the villagers must have watched cartloads of stone being hauled up the slope by horses and oxen.

their breath stinking and repelling those who try to help them. Within five days of the symptoms appearing, the victims are dead without exception. The priest himself has died within hours of attending to their spiritual needs. The village carpenter has died and there is no one to make coffins. The stinking corpses are brought out and piled up on the green, to be carted away and buried hastily outside the village by those who are left. There is no time for religious sentiment. The sheep on the green and all the village's oxen have also died. Women have to dig graves to bury their husbands and children. One woman's boils suppurate within a few days and, contrary to all expectation, she survives. Some people, for no known reason, do not fall ill at all. They call the disease 'the terrible plague' or 'the blue death', from the Latin *pestris atra* or the French *morte bleu*. Only in later ages will it be called the Black Death.

After a few terrible months, the epidemic has passed, leaving devastation in its wake. The villagers who are left alive hold a meeting on the green to count the

n Monkton, North
rkshire. The village
een is one of several
roughout England
nich have semi-
rmanent maypoles on
em.

cost, and the bailiff comes to hear their reports, so that he can tell the lord about the state of his property. Two thirds of the villagers have been wiped out. Children are left without parents, pregnant women without husbands or a midwife. The village carpenter's death has left a house half built. There is no priest to pray for the souls of the dead or give thanks for those who have survived. There are not enough men to harvest the crops, and the corn rots in the fields. Houses stand empty and grow damp for want of fires to keep them dry. The women are afraid to draw water from the well in case it is contaminated. But somehow the villagers must struggle on from day to day and try to rebuild their decimated community.

It is not long before the lord of the manor makes some important decisions. He is no longer the old soldier of former times, living in a castle and merely filling his purse from the produce of the land and the rents and fines he imposes on his tenants. He is a farmer, who lives in a new manor house built of stone like the church, and he makes his living by selling his produce to the growing populations of the towns. Now he has to reconsider his position; his labour force has been drastically reduced by the plague.

The bailiff informs the villagers that the lord is going to enclose two of the open fields and turn them into pasture for sheep. There is more profit in growing wool than in growing corn, and he will not need so many men to run his farmland. The third field will be left for the villagers to continue their ridge-and-furrow cultivation in order to provide for their families, and the field will be divided up between the remaining men and widows. A small number of men will still be required to work on the lord's land, but the rest will have to find other employment.

The handful of men left in the village meet on the green at frequent intervals to discuss their plight. Houses round the green are falling into dereliction. The men cannot afford to replace the few animals they possessed, and the lord of the manor will not provide a new plough team. They must still turn over a tenth of all their produce to the new parish priest as tithes, for the upkeep of the church. Their mood becomes ugly. How are they to survive in such conditions? They are not alone in their dismay, for word reaches them from neighbouring villages of similar murmurings of discontent, but the men in this region are of fairly submissive nature, and apart from isolated incidents, nothing much is done. At length, one or two of the men take their families to the town to live and find employment of some kind. Eventually they hear of a great rebellion of peasants in the south, and hope rises in their breasts that the king will do something to relieve their miserable conditions, but it all comes to nothing.

The villagers struggle on, and gradually life returns to a tolerable condition. The men who do not work for the lord of the manor have turned to making things

Stocks and whipping pos[t] Instruments of punishment like this disgrace the greens of many villages, which seem to regard them as quaint relics of some fondly imagined 'Merrie England'.

A Trusty Servants portrait would you see
This Emblamatic Figure well survey
The Porkers Snout not nice in diet shows
The Padlock shut no secrets he'll disclose
Patient the Ass his Masters wrath will bear
Swiftness in errand the Staggs feet declare
Loaded his Left hand apt to labour saith
The Vest his neatness Open hand his faith
Girt with his Sword his Shield upon his arm
himself and master he'll protect from harm

in signs on greens

ar left: 'The Hit or Miss'
: Penn Street,
uckinghamshire. Cricket
f earlier days shown on
ae sign outside the pub
hich doubles as the
aodern village team's
avilion.

eft: 'The Trusty Servant'
t Minstead, Hampshire.
he sign is an allegory of
ae qualities required in
ae perfect servant.

which they can sell at the markets in the town and other villages. They have pulled down the derelict houses and built new ones – still of timber or wattle-and-daub, with thatched roofs – for the slowly reviving population. The lord's employees are relatively prosperous, for if he does not pay them a reasonable wage, they can take their labour elsewhere, for there is now competition for it with the scarcity of manpower. Outside the village the men have cleared a large area of forest and have won from the lord the common right to graze their own animals on it.

The lord has obtained from the king a licence to hold markets and an annual fair on the village green, and a market cross has been set up on a stone pedestal to mark the spot where itinerant traders may assemble to sell their wares to the villagers, who now enjoy a modest purchasing power through their own efforts. Many more strangers are seen in the village than before, and this is how news travels from one parish to another. The fair comes to the village on one of the public holidays and provides much excitement for the younger folk. There are acrobats and jugglers, bear-baiting and swarthy foreigners with monkeys which perform tricks.

Even the old folk join in the festivities on the green on May Day, when the men go out into the forest and bring back a tall birch sapling to be set upon the green and decorated with garlands of flowers for the village maidens to dance round. For this is a ritual homage to nature which was celebrated in one form or another long before the church was here, to induce fertility in both the crops and the maidens.

Lanes have been made between this village and others now, where there were only well-worn tracks through woods and fields before, and the village green is further reduced in size by cutting away the grass in front of the houses to make dry paths in winter. What is more, the old simple plan of houses round the three sides of the green is barely recognizable, as new houses have been built on waste ground outwards from the green, giving the village plan the appearance of a spider's web with threads stretching out in various directions.

There are no serfs in the village now – all are free men, with vague notions of their rights under the law of the land. When they are brought before the lord of the manor for some misdemeanour, or before the church court for some moral indiscretion, they are allowed to speak in their own defence, and witnesses may be called on their behalf, though the lord's decision is still final. Stocks and a whipping post have appeared as permanent fixtures on the green. It is nothing for adults and children to turn out to see one of their neighbours bound to the post, stripped to the waist and whipped until blood runs down his bare back. It may be a young woman who has been convicted of consorting with gypsies. Or the village idiot, a poor lad who knows no better, is put into the stocks for a day for pissing in the churchyard.

ockham, Surrey. Gypsy
g-makers at the village's
ditional annual fête on
e green.

If the villagers agree with the punishment, the more aggressive among them may throw rotten vegetables at the victim in the stocks. If they think it harsh, and know that some village gossip got the victim into trouble, they may teach *her* a lesson by ducking her in the pond.

It was in 1376 that every village in the land was ordered by Edward III to maintain a set of stocks for the punishment of offenders. They may have been in use long before then, but the date of the royal decree is significant. It came a quarter of a century after the Black Death had reduced the nation's manpower by a third. The peasants were now more valuable than they had been before, and their increased value brought them some degree of independence and bargaining power. Discontent among the nobility with the government of the realm was matched by discontent among the poor with their standard of living. The Peasants' Revolt was imminent, and the maintenance of law and order was clearly becoming increasingly difficult, especially in rural areas.

Town squares, village greens and outside churchyard gates were the obvious places to erect the communal stocks, though sometimes they were made with wheels so that they could be moved to suitable places for the effective humiliation of particular wrongdoers. Many were also provided with whipping posts, with iron clamps by means of which an offender could be held by his wrists while he was flogged for his crime. As well as punishing offenders against public order and the criminal law, the stocks and whipping posts were used by the ecclesiastical courts for moral offences, such as fornication or failing to go to church.

The stocks we see reverently preserved on village greens throughout the country today are rarely medieval but are more recent replacements, since these instruments of 'justice' remained in use, almost unbelievably, for over five hundred years – well into Victorian times. The last recorded use of stocks was in 1865, but there is still a law on the statute book warning that any town which fails to maintain its stocks properly will forfeit its right to hold a market.

George Fox, founder of the Society of Friends, knew what it was like to sit in the stocks at the mercy of the local rabble, for the people of Mansfield put him there after beating him with their fists and sticks, and he sat 'some hours; and they brought dog-whips and horse-whips, threatening to whip me, and as I sate in the stocks they threw stones at me'.

The enterprising fellow who has long brewed ale for the villagers, at the back of his timber-framed house by the green, has opened one room so that travellers through the village can rest and drink there whilst their horses are watered at the pond and re-shod by the village blacksmith at the opposite side of the green, where the clanking sound of hammer on anvil is now a constant background noise in the village centre, replaced on Sundays by the clanking of inexpertly tuned church bells calling the faithful to worship.

Affairs of state have made little impression on the village hitherto, but now their effects begin to be felt a little. A redundant abbot, from a monastery which has been suppressed, becomes the new village priest. He preaches the new religion in the church, but after the king's death he reverts to the Roman faith and then, after a few years, he is thrown out and replaced. The local folk are confused, and the seeds of doubt are sown in their minds about the truth of anything these holy men tell them. Gossip on the green has it that the lord of the manor, who has remained faithful to the old religion all along, has a priest hidden under his floorboards.

There is much talk of violence, superstition and evil influences among the older folk who listen to the priests, the travellers, the bailiff, the market traders and others who bring them news. It is said that old women are being burnt to death as witches.

Some of the youngsters are now being taught to read by the priest, and they take a keen interest in the troupes of travelling players and minstrels who come to the village occasionally and perform their repertoire on the green on warm summer evenings. The elders shake their heads at this new-fangled entertainment, and tell the youngsters they should pay more attention to their lessons, and to the grotesque stone images those old masons made on the church so long ago – dire warnings of the wages of sin. But in the church itself there is a new treasure – a printed Bible. All the villagers have been to see it. It is chained to the pulpit, for the priest says it is very precious, and they can all believe it. It is the first printed thing they have seen. One old woman asks the priest how many years it took a lonely monk to print it, and remarks that he must have had writer's cramp when he had finished.

Milburn, Cumbria. The village school and playground occupy part the long, rectangular green. The school is the only building on the gre and was built in 1851.

Things are changing faster in the village than ever before. The youngsters are leaving almost to a man to live in the town, where they say there is better work for them than in the fields here. It is a time of unrest, and all the talk is of what on earth the world is coming to. There is a brief plague epidemic when the villagers are warned not to entertain strangers, but a child dies mysteriously. Itinerant preachers come and cast more doubts in the minds of those who listen to them.

A village gossip is saying that the wise woman who lives outside the village centre, who is able to cure illnesses with her herbs and other remedies, has cast a spell on one man's cows, for they have grown thin and give no milk. Then other cattle fall sick, and the men meet on the green to discuss what they should do. They have never seen such a thing before. It is not in the collective wisdom which has been passed down from generation to generation. It must be due to some new evil influence in these days of confusion. One of the men has a child – a fourteen-year-old girl – who saw the wise woman in the field with the cattle a few days before. She was muttering to herself and picking grasses and flowers. Perhaps there is something in the rumour. Two of the first cows to fall sick soon die. The men go to the clergyman for advice, and he confirms the evil existence of witches and says that everything must be done to root them out, for they are agents of the devil. Old women of the village recall that the wise woman was excommunicated many years ago by the bishop, when she was presented before the ecclesiastical court for repeatedly failing to attend church on Sundays. Her only excuse was that she had no clothes. The old farmer whose cows first fell sick was one of the churchwardens then.

The child who saw her in the field is questioned closely by the village elders. She says that the old woman saw her watching and flew away on a broomstick. The men become a mob, marching off to the wise woman's hovel. They drag her out, though she screams her innocence, and bring her to the village green, one of them fetching the priest meanwhile. Two women strip her of her rags and search her body for the marks of her familiars. Then her hands and feet are tied together with ropes, and the men throw her into the pond, using the ropes to drag her through it slowly. She is brought out, an emaciated old woman, dripping, choking and shivering. The women round the pond are all shouting that she floated in the water and

is a witch. The clergyman has doubts, but the villagers are in ugly mood, and he dare not resist them. He orders the old woman to be taken to the bishop for trial, and sends the villagers back to their homes. A few days later they hear that the old woman has been burnt at the stake in the town square that was once a village green like theirs. Many years later, when the teenage girl has grown up, she will deny ever saying such an absurd thing as that the old woman flew away on a broomstick.

Printed newsletters now find their way to the village occasionally, and by this means the people learn of matters of moment in the capital, which have little effect on their daily lives at present – an attempt to blow up parliament; civil war; the execution of the king. But soon soldiers come and smash images in the village

ar memorials on greens

ove left: Collingbourne
cis, Wiltshire.

ove: Zeals, Wiltshire.

ove right: Guiting
wer, Gloucestershire.

church, and the people are forbidden to erect a maypole on May Day, since the government has decreed that such things are wicked pagan practices. One Puritan fanatic has attacked the age-old tradition whereby men and women, boys and girls go off into the woods the night before May Day to indulge in carefree revelries the whole night long in thanksgiving for the new spring. 'I have heard it credibly reported,' Philip Stubbes wrote, 'by men of great gravity and reputation, that of forty, threescore or a hundred maids going to the wood over night, there have scarcely the third part of them returned home again undefiled.' This, of course, is the wild exaggeration of a propagandist with no sympathy for country matters. He who can see only evil in the old pagan spring festivities is too good for this world, and Stubbes was not long in leaving it.

Along with the maypole, the local Morris men, who were to be seen dancing in the churchyard and around the green on May Day and other festivals, with their figures dressed up as Robin Hood, Maid Marian and others, have also been banned as pagan and immoral. And no one is allowed to play games on the green on the Sabbath, despite the fact that some folk can remember the vicar reading out from his pulpit a proclamation from King James which said: 'For when shall the common people have leave to exercise, if not upon the Sundays and holidays, seeing they must apply their labour and win their living in all working days?'

There is much head-wagging at such interference with old traditions, but other changes have occurred which are more welcome. For some years past a great deal of rebuilding has been going on in the village. The houses round the green are no longer the timber hovels they have been for so many centuries, but are built with bricks and mortar and have two floors, with rooms for sleeping in up flights of steps, and chimneys and tiled roofs instead of thatch, so that there will not be so many fires. The old thatch-hook, which has always been kept on the wall of the church, is rarely used nowadays.

The ale-house is now called the Horseshoe Inn, and strangers may sleep as well as drink there, and stables are provided for their horses. The blacksmith is one of the most prosperous men in the village, but the baker is also doing well and keeps stocks of butter and cheese and milk, as well as bread, so that the villagers can buy them at any time they choose. The old well on the green has been replaced by a modern pump, making it much easier and quicker to draw water, though the women still gather round it for their daily gossip.

Soon a new king is on the throne, and children can dance round the maypole again, but Sundays are quieter than they used to be. People walk on the green and sit on it on summer evenings outside the inn, but the men no longer play football on it or take their fighting cocks to the hollow at the farthest corner from the church and make bets as they gather round in a noisy and excited circle to watch the mains. The vicar is forever crashing his fist down on the pulpit and telling the villagers that they are miserable sinners, and he has even tried to stop the annual fair on the green, but a deputation of villagers went to see the squire at the big house, and he intervened on their behalf to save the fair, persuading the vicar that it is harmless enough and brings trade to the village.

The squire and his lady are popular with the villagers. They not only provide work on their estate but give money to the poor, and the lady visits sick children. There is talk of building a school in the village, and it will be on the green, right at the centre of things, for the safety and convenience of the children. Although the villagers have fiercely resisted any building on their green for centuries, they

Tittersham, Kent. A cricket match in progress around the middle of the nineteenth century, with village church and oast houses forming the background to an oil painting attributed to Charles Deane. Note the underarm bowler.

May Day in Merrie England. Dancing round the maypole erected on a village green with church and manor house close by. An engraving by J. Nash.

will not object to a school, for that is something to be proud of and is a gift to the villagers themselves, not something for the benefit of a rich landowner.

Those village men who are still farmers now have their own fields, enclosed by hedges and with trees to provide shelter for their livestock. But even those who are not farmers grow their own vegetables in their gardens and have apple trees there and grow flowers at the fronts of their houses overlooking the green, and it becomes a matter of community pride for them to cut the grass on the green and not let it grow wild as it used to.

Soon the children have a new village tradition to grow up with – a big bonfire on the green on 5 November each year, when they make an effigy of Guy Fawkes and burn it with much shouting and merriment. These children have never seen a *real* person burnt, so they have no conception of the horror their play represents, just as they do not understand the symbolic eroticism involved in dancing round the maypole.

Some years pass, and there is great anger and excitement in the village when the new squire, a young man who spends nearly all his time in the city and hardly ever speaks to the villagers, announces that he intends to enclose the green as part of his farmland, and graze his sheep on it. Labourers come from the town and begin to put up fences round the green, leaving only the pond and a small area round the pump free. The village men hold angry meetings at the inn and decide on a course of action. During the night they all gather and pull the fences down again. Every post is pulled up by the morning.

The squire reads the riot act to the villagers via his estate manager and puts the fences up again, but the villagers take him to court, and after a long legal battle they win, the squire being told that he does not have the right to enclose the village green, which is the common property of the inhabitants.

And so the story goes on. The passing decades see the surfacing of the roads and the erection of a signpost directing travellers to neighbouring villages; the administration of the green by a parish council instead of the redundant squire; the appearance of street lights round the green; the erection of a war memorial to the villagers who lost their lives in the First World War; the preservation of the disused pump by building a little shelter over it; the demolition of the former black-smith's forge to make way for a petrol filling station; the discreet edging of the green's circumference with white posts to prevent motorists parking their cars on it, and so on. It is time for us to leave this distillation of village history and go in search of real greens, each with its own history and character to add to the cumulative story of the village greens of England.

III

The South East

VILLAGE GREENS OF KENT, SUSSEX, SURREY AND GREATER LONDON

The green at Offham in Kent, not far from Maidstone, bears a famous symbol of the one-time importance of village greens as the cradles of England's military prowess. It is a quintain, or tilting pole, which was used by medieval knights and their squires for practice of horsemanship and the bearing of arms. The green is of irregular shape and modest size, but it was large enough for mounted men to ride full tilt at the pole with lances outstretched to score a hit against the extended patterned board. But there was a sting in the tail of this target. The pivoted arm of the quintain had a sandbag at its other end, and when the target was struck, the bag swung round and dealt a hefty blow to the unwary horseman as he rode by. Medieval target practice would thus have afforded much merriment to the village spectators, cheering the skilful knights who were adept at dodging the sandbag, and falling about with laughter at the inexperienced young squires who were unceremoniously knocked off their horses. Young local riders still re-live this medieval custom on occasion. Needless to say, perhaps, one of the houses surrounding the green is called Quintain House – an early eighteenth-century house of chequered brickwork – but this is hop-growing country, and village greens here are often accompanied by oast-houses with their familiar white cowls, often nowadays converted into dwelling houses.

Although the quintain at Offham is unique, the green is characteristic of Kent in other respects. The greens here vary in size but are mostly on the Weald, and appear to be clearings in the original forest, round the circumference of which the first settlers built their huts. But it is often the case in Kent that the village church is some distance away from the green, and if we ask the 'chicken or egg' question in regard to them, it seems evident here – as it does not elsewhere – that the green

ham, Kent. The
intain on the green is a
ique survival of
dieval military training.

was here before the church. The stand-offish attitude of the church was perhaps provoked by the pagan associations of the green.

It has been said that the largest village green in Kent is at Stelling Minnis, south of Canterbury. Its extent is about ninety acres, but its status as a village green has been challenged, and it is claimed as a common, in private ownership. The village itself is now absorbed in Upper Hardres. Several other Kentish greens are subject to common rights, such as those at Edenbridge, Lamberhurst and Meopham. The latter's green bears a windmill, but paradoxically Meopham is a street village rather than a green one, and its church is sited at the north end of its long main road.

Otford and Groombridge are villages which perhaps come closer to meeting the requirements most people have in their imaginations when thinking of typical green villages. They are of similar size, Groombridge's sloping triangular green slightly the larger of the two, but Otford's, which has a pond in it, has been split up by a road junction. Both greens have the village church comfortably close by, as does the green in the attractive village of Boxley, along with the village pub.

The sloping and tapered green at Westerham, with the church at one end, is highly unusual in sporting statues of two national heroes. Statues are scarce enough even in the provincial towns and cities of England, so to find a *village* with two signifies something out of the ordinary, and Westerham is to be congratulated. The older statue is of General James Wolfe, the victor of Quebec, who was born here in 1727. The newer one is of Sir Winston Churchill, who was a local resident at Chartwell for nearly half a century apart from his temporary absences in Downing Street. The green at Knockholt, very tidy, is at the centre of Kent's highest village and has contributed to its election in the past as the county's best-kept village.

The classic green of this area of Kent is perhaps that at Meopham Green, sometimes called Pitfield Green. It lies half a mile or so south of the larger village of Meopham and has at its centre a triangular green, the chief modern use of which is attested to by the name of the village pub, 'The Cricketers'. There is also a war memorial at one corner.

Hook Green, Culverstone Green, Fawkham Green, Dunton Green and Goose Green are among the sites on that side of the Medway where the Kentish Men are traditionally distinguished from the Men of Kent across the river, but the mere survival of the name 'Green' is not an infallible guide to the presence of a green today, and even when there is a green, it may well be a common. Many villages that once had greens now have little squares, and the attractive villages of Shere and Chilham are among those in Kent which once had greens. This also applies to other parts of the country, as we shall see. But one place in Kent deserves mention for introducing new greens to the county, though it has introduced less welcome features as well. New Ash Green was developed as a new 'urban' village with government approval in the late sixties, with communal open spaces which were made the responsibility of the residents' societies in a bid to foster a community spirit. Policy changes and financial problems meant that the original conception of what New Ash Green should be like has not been fully realized, but the place is interesting as a variation on the usual theme of village greens of ancient origin, such as those at Shipbourne, very large and uneven, and Matfield Green, with its duckpond. Both of these are regarded as commons.

The pub at Horsmonden, well over on the eastern side of the Medway, is called 'The Gun', and by the edge of the green outside stands a cannon cast by John Browne, whose trade gave the pub its name, for he was a designer of firearms for both Charles I and Cromwell, his guns being made of the Wealden iron that gave the district much of its prosperity before the Industrial Revolution, and which reminds us that one of the most familiar neighbours of English village greens at one time was the blacksmith's forge, now – alas – practically extinct. The Flying Horse on the green at Boughton Lees may have been named from the fairground horses there on annual fair day, for it is unlikely that such an adjective would have been applied to the animals carrying travellers through the village on the Pilgrims' Way.

Woodchurch is another village with a more-or-less triangular green at its centre, keeping close company with the church. Bearsted's church is separate from the village centre, but the green here is quite large, like the one at Woodchurch, and is noted for the fact that Alfred Mynn, one of the great early figures of the cricketing records, played on it. He was known as 'the Lion of Kent'. He stood over six feet tall and weighed seventeen stone, and was the first fast round-arm bowler, who 'dug a grave' with his left foot if the ground was soft. It needed a sizeable green for him to bowl on, and Bearsted's is an epitome of village England, with houses and trees lining the green where the slight slope has aided many a quickish bowler since Mynn's day. (Kent has some claim to being the chief surviving home of village cricket today; among other notable cricketing greens is the one at East Malling.) The green at Bearsted, however, has a more important historical association than its cricket. Here in 1381 Wat Tyler assembled his followers in the Peasants' Revolt, to join up with the men of Essex in their march to London in that short-lived demonstration against feudal oppression.

West Peckham is another village well known for cricket on its two-acre green, where modern villagers have played the game in the shadow of the Norman church with its squat Saxon tower as they did in 1800, when the local paper announced:

Westerham, Kent. The statue of Sir Winston Churchill by Oscar Nemon was presented to the village by Yugoslavia and is the most recent addition to the green.

This is to give Notice
That on Whit-Thursday, being the Fair-Day,
there will be a
MATCH OF CRICKET
PLAYED on WEST PECKHAM sporting place,
between the gentlemen of Meopham against
the gentlemen of East Peckham, for a
Guinea each Man.

Matches like this drew large crowds of spectators, and many of them, in Kent at least, would watch the game standing in hop waggons drawn up round the ground.

There was plenty of lively betting on cricket in the game's early days, and the 'gentlemen' (whose amateur status entitled them, until relatively recently, to have

t: West Peckham, Kent.
e village cricket pitch is
ed off on the green with
Norman church beside

their initials printed *before* their surnames on the score sheets and in the newspapers, instead of *after*, like the professional players) often made a fair bit on the side and were sometimes even bribed to lose a game. The curious snobbery of cricket lasted until a few years ago in some quarters, in spite of the fact that the village game was a powerful force in breaking down class barriers, bringing the squire and the nobleman together with their social inferiors, such as the publican and the black-smith, to work together as a team.

On the other side of Tonbridge, Leigh has a green which qualifies, at seven acres, as one of Kent's largest. It has the cricket pitch which is almost obligatory in this county, and the village church stands solidly above it, but road signs and other paraphernalia intrude too much for it to be counted among the most attractive greens of Kent.

Benenden's green also has a cricket pitch, as well as chestnut trees and tile-hung cottages beside it. William Cobbett recommended that the village stocks should be occupied by a Methodist parson he heard preaching there.

The diminutive green at Biddenden is only big enough to support a few shrubs and the famous village sign showing the Biddenden Maids, the Siamese twins Eliza and Mary Chalkhurst, who started a local charity by leaving to the poor a plot of ground now known as 'Bread and Cheese Land'.

ht: Biddenden, Kent.
e sign on the green
ws the famous
denden Maids,
tedly Siamese twins
o lived here in the
eenth century and
nded a local charity.

Bosham, West Sussex. Quay Meadow lies at the water's edge in Chichester Harbour and has all the virtues of a village green, with the parish church behind it.

Hawkhurst might be called a small town, and this is perhaps the time to say that places which have grown into towns often still have their original greens qualifying for mention in this book, though they may no longer be at the centre of community life. Hawkhurst's green is known as 'the Moor', and from it the more modern part of the village stretches out into the street village end known as Highgate.

The eastern end of Kent around Canterbury has one or two greens to show, and that at Wickhambreaux is the most picturesque. It is triangular and is shaded by lime trees and chestnuts, and round it are attractive cottages, rectory, post office, an avenue leading to the church, and a weatherboarded water-mill still in working order.

Romney Marsh is not a place to look for village greens, for the same reason as their absence in the fens of eastern England, but already as we pass from Kent into Sussex we have noticed some of the most characteristic and charming elements of England's village greens – their variety of size and shape; the peculiar uses to which they have been put; and their uniqueness, for no two greens are exactly alike. More than the vernacular architecture around it, or the adjacent village church or pub, a green is the heart of its respective village, from which one may form an instant impression of the character of the place. If it is well looked after, it is still the nucleus of a happy rural community; if not, it is likely to be a redundant bit of ground in an outward-looking village hankering after urbanism, and only remains there because no one knows what else to do with it.

East and West Sussex have between them more than fifty village greens with a variation in size ranging from the fifteen-acre green at Heyshott, near Midhurst, to the mere quarter-of-an-acre at Turners Hill, near Crawley. The incidence of village greens is higher in the two halves of Sussex than in Kent, but the average size smaller, whereas when we come to Surrey, the incidence is much higher than in either Sussex or Kent, and the average size much greater.

The green at Northiam in East Sussex is not the county's smallest, but at less than half an acre it is hardly of impressive size. It should not be missed on that account, however, for what it lacks in acreage, it makes up for in illustrious association. It is of triangular shape, among the village's weatherboarded houses, and has upon it an ancient oak tree which shaded queen Elizabeth I in August 1573 when she came here and left a pair of shoes behind as a memento.

Ewhurst's green has the church of St James on one side and weatherboarded houses facing it on the other, and it is certainly difficult to believe such greens as this ever were designed to have a defensive function.

The map of Sussex is sprinkled with greens whose names we have not the space to enquire into but which are transparently part of that inward-looking parochial way of life which had no great concern with the outside world before the Industrial Revolution, even though so close to London – Oxley's Green, Partridge Green, Shover's Green, Woodmansgreen, Posey Green, Stunts Greens, Gospel Green, Bells Yew Green, Snow Hill Green, *et al.*

Sedlescombe has a long triangular green slightly larger than Northiam's, complete with ornate village pump and flanked by stylish houses, whilst to the south-west, on the coast near Brighton, Rottingdean's small green is very attractive, with a village pond and one or two notable houses nearby. Sir Edward Burne-Jones lived here, at North End House, for the last eighteen years of his life, and loved the peaceful village, but Rudyard Kipling, who stayed with the Burne-Joneses and later rented a house called 'The Elms', which stood 'like an island' in the green, soon found the village overpopulated, and the tourists who came to gape got on his nerves, despite the high wall round the property. The green was the scene of some excitement when the Boer War ended, for Lady Burne-Jones hung out a black flag at the Boer capitulation, and Kipling had to rush across the green to rescue her from angry young demonstrators who were threatening to set fire to a hedge in order to burn the flag down. Kipling, who had founded a boys' club in the village, left soon afterwards, when he purchased Bateman's.

Ringmer has a large green on which the village sign records its association with Gulielma Springett, among other notabilities. Gulielma was born in this village, the daughter of Sir John and Lady Mary Springett, and she became the wife of William Penn, the Quaker and founder of Pennsylvania.

Newick's triangular green is accompanied by the pub, 'The Bull', but here we are not concerned with the usual farm animal that is to be found among the Red Cows throughout England. Because Newick lay on the Pilgrims' Way to Canterbury, this bull is of the papal variety. The green itself supports a Victorian village pump with a lion's head as the spout.

The tiny triangular green on the chalk at East Dean is surrounded by flint cottages, whilst at Southease the church is of flint and stands on the green – a Norman building of unknown dedication with a round tower surmounted by a conical roof.

Frant lies close to the Kent border and has a spacious green at the centre of a village standing high up near Tunbridge Wells and having fine views. The seven-acre green is interesting for still having the old village archery butts on it.

Withyham's green is at the centre of a scattered village whose lords of the manor from the thirteenth century were the Sackville family, and their impressive monuments are in the village church. Staplefield, meanwhile, has its church beside a large green with the Jolly Tanners inn among the Victorian houses round it.

Across the border in West Sussex, Horsted Keynes takes the second part of its

Abinger Hammer, Surrey. The long green forms the banks of the stream through a village which takes its name from the water-driven hammers of the old iron industry.

name from the medieval de Cahanges lords of the manor, whose church stands in a hollow below the acre-and-a-half of green which is surrounded by Tudor houses and two pubs.

Ebernoe is a tiny, unspoiled village with a long tradition kept up on Horn Fair Day, which is 25 July. A cricket match takes place (weather permitting) as well as the fair, and a horned sheep is roasted on a spit to be shared among those present. The batsman making the highest score in the match is given a horn as a souvenir. The green, however, is actually a common.

Lovers of cricket and the literature of cricket will be aware that Storrington was the model for Tillingfold in the cricket stories of Hugh de Selincourt, who captained the Storrington side in his day. But alas, Storrington does not have a village green now, and did not then, for the author refers to the team meeting in the village square for their transport to away matches.

For sheer contrast in size to Ebernoe's green, Wisborough Green is unbeatable in this vicinity. It is huge – eleven acres – and lined with trees. Several irregular extensions reach out from the formality of the main rectangular shape, one of them leading to the village church, and it is an interesting though unanswerable question whether one of the extensions was, in fact, the original green. Chilgrove's green is also long, though not half so large as Wisborough's. The hamlet is tucked below the South Downs near Singleton, and the green has the village pub as neighbour.

One of the most unusual greens in Sussex, and indeed in all south-east England, is at Bosham, overlooking Chichester Harbour. Right at the water's edge is Quay Meadow, sometimes described simply as a 'field', but whatever its legal status, it has all the merits of a village green and is preserved by the National Trust as such. Some say this is where Canute, or Cnut, the great Dane, effectively demonstrated that there are limits to kingly power by ordering the incoming tide to recede, but even if you don't believe it, call the place Bos-ham, not Bosh-am.

Tennyson makes Thomas à Becket refer to Bosham's 'sea-creek – the pretty rill that falls into it – the green field – the gray church . . .', and the grey church still stands behind the green field on the site of what was perhaps the earliest church in Sussex, which is depicted in the Bayeux Tapestry, for King Harold prayed here before travelling to Normandy. There was much to-ing and fro-ing at this harbour by the Saxon kings and earls of Wessex, as the Anglo-Saxon Chronicle makes clear, and it may be that Quay Meadow has been trod by more English noblemen than any other village green in the land.

Lurgashall and Lickfold, neighbours in the country north of Midhurst, have greens of more or less equal size, both triangular and both very attractive, with some nice buildings round them. Lurgashall's name is significant, if the conjectures of the place-name experts are correct, for it comes from the Old English *lytel goers-healh*, which means 'little grazing land'.

Fletching's green, near Petworth, may be a common, but its 2½ acres are characteristic of local greens, and the name is interesting, indicating a medieval association with arrow-makers like the village further east and being derived from the French *flèche*.

When we come to Tinsley Green, we are almost in Surrey, and although the place seems nearly part of Gatwick Airport runway, it is noted for a more ancient sound than jet aircraft taking off – the click of colliding glass balls – for it is the scene of the annual marbles championship held in a ring outside the Greyhound Inn. 'Marbles Day' was traditionally Good Friday, for on village greens throughout Surrey and Sussex the game's season was throughout Lent, and what is now regarded as the world marbles championship continues a custom at Tinsley Green that is three centuries old.

Lamb's Green, just the other side of Crawley, manages to keep its distance from the new town which has absorbed Gossops Green, Langley Green and West Green since the Second World War, but Surrey is still today one of the most heavily wooded counties of England. Its multitude of village greens began as clearings in the forests when the Saxon invaders commenced their settlement of the area, and in some cases this impression of a clearing still remains, as if the ideas of the Saxons have remained valid for fifteen centuries. The name-ending '-fold' means 'forest clearing', and at Chiddingfold the large, irregular green, complete with duckpond and surrounded by church, Crown Inn, manor house and brick and tile cottages, is a classic example of the green village in this part of the country. The Crown claims to be the oldest licensed house in England, and though there are plenty of other claimants to that title, there has been an inn here since the late thirteenth century; it is said that Edward VI slept in it. Chiddingfold was famous as a glassmaking centre in medieval times, and 'mine host' at the inn supplied ale not only to quench the thirst of the glassmakers but also to wash the glass in, for ale was reckoned to harden the product.

The other local industry was iron, and from this Abinger Hammer gets its name, from the water-driven hammers in the local forges. It is one of a pair of villages, the other being Abinger Common, and whilst the common there looks like a triangular village green, with church, inn and manor house around it, the green at Abinger Hammer might be taken for a common, as the houses face a long five-acre expanse of green with a stream running through it. Abinger might seem almost perverse in clinging to its ancient rural heritage, for it not only preserves its village stocks and whipping post but is one of those places where local children still dance round a maypole on May Day. The maypole is erected and garlanded on the green at Abinger Hammer, and here, at the very threshold of the parish church, is enacted a blatantly pagan ritual which the Church, having failed to suppress or absorb, has perforce to tolerate.

Before 1644, when Parliament banned what the Puritans saw as a 'stinckynge idoll', people all over England would go into the woods on the last day of April and cut down birch saplings (easily found here in Surrey) to drag back to their greens to be erected and dressed in readiness for the following day's celebration of spring fertility. In some parts, hawthorn was apparently used, despite the fact that it is supposed to be an unlucky tree, and in others, a semi-permanent pole was kept on the village green to be painted and decorated each year and renewed when the foot of the pole had rotted. Permanent maypoles would often be of enormous size, dragged from the woods by oxen, and a few villages – as we shall see – still keep permanent maypoles on their greens, for these communal phallic symbols soon reappeared everywhere after the Restoration, and never entirely vanished even during the years of the Commonwealth, when May Day was abolished and all maypoles were to be 'taken down and removed by the constables and church wardens of the parish'. Expressions of joy at the coming of spring are too deeply embedded to be easily suppressed, and at Abinger Hammer we can see the survival – somewhat refined maybe – of a spontaneous celebration which stretches back to the religion of the Roman occupation and was certainly practised by the Saxons in what is now north Germany. The children who innocently worship the symbolic phallus by plaiting it with coloured streamers as they dance round it in two interweaving circles are carrying on an age-old ritual intended to ensure the fertility of women, animals and soil.

A more common preoccupation on the greens of Surrey from May onwards is village cricket, which likewise scandalized the Puritans when played on Sundays. But then, those blinkered bigots disapproved of everything that occurred on village greens except the humiliation of some poor unfortunate in the stocks. On the greens at Godstone and Brockham, Ockley and Thursley and Tilford and many others, the gentlemen and players come out in their whites on weekend afternoons to enjoy what has rightly been called the finest team game ever invented by man. The setting at Brockham Green is most familiar, having been much photographed over the years. The green here is triangular, and the pitch where W. G. Grace once batted is overlooked by church, cottages and trees, with Box Hill rising in the background.

Although the distinction of cradling the modern game belongs to Hampshire, where the Hambledon Club formulated the rules and organization of the cricket we know today, the village greens of Kent and Surrey were certainly the scenes

...urton, Wiltshire.

...st Hanney,
...fordshire. Greens tend
...get smaller the farther
... travels from the south
...wards the Midlands.

of some of the earliest matches, though we should scarcely recognize them as the game we are now so familiar with. Cricket is said to have been played in Surrey in the sixteenth century. The bowlers then would have aimed the ball with an under-arm throw at wickets defended by batsmen with curved bats, and their runs would have been recorded by notches cut in a stick. The actual origins of the game are obscure but clearly ancient, and from the holiday afternoon amusement of working men on village greens gradually evolved the international five-day test matches which are the highest pinnacles of the modern game. But it is interesting that cricket has come full circle, and a return to the one-day match in which a high run rate is the order of the day has brought the first-class cricket grounds back to an echo of the time-honoured village green game. Kennington Oval, one of the two or three finest cricket grounds in England, is the offspring of Surrey's village greens, and the professional cricketers who play there are the heirs in spirit of the village blacksmith, bricklayer, farmer, postman, cobbler and other locals who, captained by the squire or the schoolmaster, vacated the pavilion or the pub after lunch to take on the opposition and provide the local talking-point for the following week.

The village pub at Ockley is 'The Cricketers', but unlike the one at Brockham, the green itself is long and irregular, with a road running along one side and attractive timber-framed or weatherboarded houses on the other, with Leith Hill shading them from the west. The village pump survives here. Ockley's green is subject to common rights, but Ewhurst's is not. The green here, as so often, is some distance from the church, so it is probably not the original centre of the village. William Cobbett, a native of Farnham, thought Ewhurst a very pretty village and describes riding through the Weald's deep clay lanes between it and Ockley after being warned about the difficulty of the road for horses. Horses are a familiar sight on the green itself in November, when the hunting season commences, whilst at the same time many greens, such as Brockham's, are noted for their bonfires and firework displays.

Cobbett had much to say in his *Rural Rides* about Godstone, which hangs on to its village character despite its proximity to the metropolis. The green is square and has one of several ponds in the village, with the pub opposite this one. Cobbett was impressed by the neat gardens and the flowers growing in them, and remarked on the fact that hops were grown there, between the ridges of chalk and sand running by it in east-west direction.

Leigh is on the Lower Greensand on the south side of the River Mole, and its pub and old village school face each other across the green, which is neat and triangular and has the church at its apex among weatherboarded cottages, as well as the village pump on it, housed beneath a tiled and attractively lichened roof of four gables supported on oak posts.

The green is in the eastern half of this stylish village of brown ironstone.

On the south-east side of Guildford, Shalford and Shamley Green offer contrasts we soon become used to in Surrey. Shalford's green is a fair-sized one of irregular shape with a suburban look about it, whilst Shamley Green is a series of triangular shapes linking up into a large area which is subject to common rights and has some attractive cottages round it. Ellen's Green is large, in the southernmost corner of this county where greens are – if you will pardon the expression – common as well as plentiful, more greens being subject to rights of commonage here than those that are not. The green at Elstead, however, is small and triangular, with a medieval stone bridge across the stream nearby and some good farm buildings and cottages around it.

Buckland and Walton-on-the-Hill, near Reigate and Leatherhead respectively, present contrasts in their greens, too. Buckland's is an informal three-acre green with a round pond on it and some farm buildings among the houses, as well as the village church. It still looks completely rural, whilst the green at Walton-on-the-Hill, strictly geometrical and with white posts round its perimeter, has a distinctly suburban look. The lych-gate into the churchyard is at one corner, among a mixture of Georgian, Victorian and more recent houses.

Woodcote village is unashamedly a suburb, created entirely at the turn of the century by William Webb, who set out to create an estate in which 'Garden First' was the guiding principle, the philosophy being that the garden was more important than the house within it, and in fact the gardens and layout of the estate were

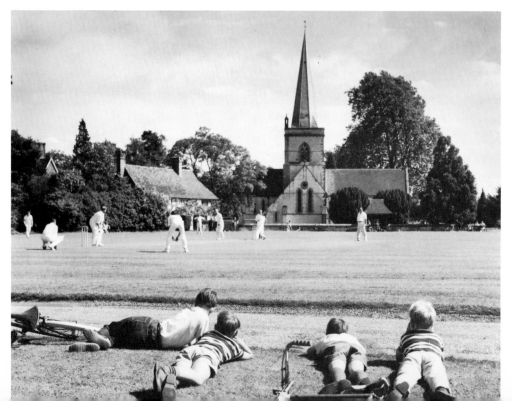

Brockham, Surrey. A familiar view of the triangular green where Dr W. G. Grace once played. Except for the bicycles, the scene has hardly changed since his day.

created before the houses were even begun. The 'village' became a fashionable residential area for city commuters and professional men. So far, so good, but everyone who has any concern with Woodcote ought to be thoroughly ashamed of the imported stocks and whipping post on the green, attempting to give the village an antiquity which is entirely bogus and which ought to be removed by public demand as a tasteless phoney.

The green at Esher is so full of traffic and parked vehicles nowadays that it is hard to appreciate the qualities of this open area of suburban Surrey, but there is a war memorial on one side, with the church and cottages, as well as more modern houses, and the entrance gates to Esher Place, the former palace of a bishop of Winchester, though little remains of it now.

Cobham has a green with blossom trees on it and the Running Mare public house facing it. The name may refer to an ancient harvest ritual, for the harvest was as much a time for celebration in the arable farming villages of England, where greens proliferate, as was May Day. In some parts of Europe, including the Home Counties of England, the last blades of corn left to be cut were tied together and called 'the mare'. Reapers threw their sickles at it until one of them cut it, and it was then sent on to a farmer whose corn had not yet been cut, for it represented the captured corn spirit, and it could not be killed until the whole harvest was completed – hence the running mare.

At Cobham and Esher, you could hardly play cricket without breaking windows,

Walton-on-the-Hill, Surrey. A winter's view of this formal green perilously close to London's grasping tentacles.

Paddington Green, London. The fine statue of the actress Sarah Siddons as the Tragic Muse was unveiled in 1897, sixty-six years after her burial in the adjoining churchyard.

but Englefield Green, near the Berkshire border, is a huge area of thirty-four acres, naturally subject to common rights.

Tilford and Thursley both have greens with cricket pitches. Tilford's is a largish triangular green with a medieval stone bridge crossing the River Wey on the eastern side. This may have been built by the monks of Waverley Abbey, the first Cistercian house in England, the ruins of which stand a mile to the north. Thursley's green is smaller but has wide views to the north as far as the Hog's Back. Cobbett had admired the oak tree on Tilford's green, having seen it grow from the time when he was a small boy to its full maturity when he wrote *Rural Rides*. But Thursley's green now has an acacia tree which was planted in his memory, and quite right, too, for no village in England ever got more tantalizing publicity than Cobbett gave this little place, through a determination to get here and see it despite being constantly warned that there was no road to it.

Brook, Hambledon and Old Coulsdon are among the many other attractive village greens of Surrey. As we move towards Greater London I am tempted to mention Ham, which, although it has what is actually a common, has all the appearance of a large village green, with pond and pub and houses lining it on three sides, many of them being of the elegant Georgian type we should expect on what was then a rural area within a gentleman's convenient ride by coach from London.

Nor should Kew be overlooked in any exploration of English village greens. It is now an urban area of Greater London but was a rural village not so long ago, much favoured by royalty, and its triangular green, now bisected by the Kew Bridge road leading south from the Thames, has St Anne's Church standing on it and stylish Georgian houses around it. The entrance to the Royal Botanic Gardens is at one corner. In the churchyard is the grave of Thomas Gainsborough, the favourite court painter of the same royal personages who made Kew so fashionable. He was buried there quietly, at his own request, close to his lifelong friend Joshua Kirby, in the presence of Sir Joshua Reynolds, Richard Brinsley Sheridan and many others. Several men of more recent fame have shared a love for what was once the peacefulness of Kew Green, so conveniently situated for those whose daily business was in London.

Some of the best village greens in the south-east are, in fact, in London itself. On the Surrey side of the river, Mortlake's green is square, and Barnes Green is a dogleg-shaped extension of Barnes Common, with a large pond in it. The names alone are enough to tell us that Parsons Green and Goose Green, though they may now be called 'urban open spaces', are the original centres of villages long ago swallowed up in the irresistible growth of the capital. Parsons Green, in the borough of Hammersmith, is of the classic triangular shape and has Georgian houses facing it from the time when London's embracing tentacles started to reach out towards it.

A good many places in London where 'green' is retained in the name have, naturally enough, been built on or turned into surfaced squares, but we can still trace many sites of what were once village greens. Clerkenwell Green, where my publisher's offices stand, is a case where the green has long since vanished but the open space remains, in front of the church. Deptford Green, long ago built over, was at the heart of a fishing village in the country when the poet and dramatist Christopher Marlowe was killed there, either in a tavern brawl or, as some say, because he was a government spy. He was buried in the churchyard which over-looked the green and is now itself overlooked by a power station.

Bethnal Green still remains at the original centre of one of the so-called Tower Hamlets, well outside London until the nineteenth century, and Turnham Green at Chiswick is of irregular shape with town hall, church and fire station round it. Paddington was still a quiet village in the fields a century and a half ago: its green still remains, though much changed. What remains is irregular in shape and lies, railed in, just off the Edgware Road, with a statue of the actress Sarah Siddons on it. She had lived here and was buried in the churchyard of the adjacent yellow brick church of St Mary. The statue was unveiled by Sir Henry Irving sixty-six years after her death, which occurred two years after the first regular omnibus service into the City was started from this green by George Shillibeer. The fare from Pad-dington Green to the Bank was a shilling, and you got a free newspaper to read on the way.

Newington was well known to Edgar Allan Poe, who lived there from 1817 to 1820, and he called it 'a misty looking village of England' then. It is hardly that now, but its railed-in green survives, more or less oblong in shape.

Middlesex was a county well endowed with village greens, and although some, such as Palmers Green and Golders Green, have been lost in its swallowing up by London, several remain. Norwood's is quite large and triangular, whilst Southgate's is small and split up by roadways into irregular shapes like pieces of a jigsaw puzzle. Ealing and Enfield still have the remnants of their former village greens, while Strand-on-the-Green, on the opposite bank of the Thames from Kew, though best known for its riverside elegance, has a more or less square green only a few yards from the waterfront.

IV

The Heartland of Green Villages

HERTFORDSHIRE, BUCKINGHAMSHIRE AND ESSEX

Nearly a fifth of all the village greens of England occur in the three counties dealt with in this chapter. Why is it that this strip of country bordering London on its north side should have such a concentration of our remaining green villages? The reasons are no doubt to do with both social and political history.

Firstly, the three counties form an area that was not so heavily influenced by Scandinavian settlement as the counties to the north of them. Only Essex was within the Danelaw, and Anglo-Saxon customs remained relatively untouched and free to assert themselves in new settlements. This is, of course, just as true of the counties south of London, but the second reason isolates these northern Home Counties somewhat. The relatively flat clay of the London Basin, on which the three counties chiefly lay, gave them a predominantly arable farming economy, and so, if the theory that green villages are related to the open field feudal system is correct, settlement in Hertfordshire, Buckinghamshire and Essex would have been more regularly on the classic Anglo-Saxon pattern, with an open space – usually triangular – left among the peasants' dwellings for use as a market space, as a meeting place and possibly for protection of such livestock as the villagers possessed – probably no more than a few geese in these villages.

There is, however, a complicated sub-plot to this scenario, for although Hertfordshire, in particular, has such a large number of greens, few of them are at the centre of nucleated villages. What seems to have happened is that small farming settlements grew up over a long period in clearings of the thick forest that still covered the area when the Romans departed. Some settlements continued in occupation from the Roman period onward, but instead of continuous expansion of these existing hamlets, Anglo-Saxon settlers cleared fresh areas nearby and generated dispersed hamlets, in which a green might be in one quarter but the new Christian church

erleaf: Aldbury,
rtfordshire. The green
the centre of this village
low the Chilterns is
gely occupied by the
ckpond. The building
th the tall chimney is
e former village
kehouse.

in another. Thus the region is one of 'Ends' and 'Greens', and the environs of a modern village may embrace more than one green, as at Clavering in Essex, which has three, and Sandon in Hertfordshire, which has no fewer than nine.

This fragmentation is what gives rural Hertfordshire so much of its charm, with quiet and very narrow lanes linking the scattered hamlets. Weston, near Hitchin, is a case in point. Scattered along narrow lanes in all directions from the centre of the modern village are Church End, Green End, Damask Green, Hall's Green and Warren's Green.

Sarratt, on the fringe of the Chiltern Hills near Rickmansworth, has a green which is untypical in being unusually long and narrow, but in other respects the village is characteristic of the western part of the county. Its ancient flint church, which has Roman brick in it, stands some distance away from the green, at what is naturally known as Church End, and the county historian Chauncy, writing at the end of the seventeenth century, said that the church was at the centre of the village.

But it is not so now. The centre has shifted to the green, which has the village shops on one side of it, as well as houses all round it in a hotch-potch of architectural styles. Half a mile up the road is a small triangular green called Rosehall Green, with a wood across the road which contains the rectangular earthwork of a pre-historic homestead, and another wood behind in which is the supposed site of the manor house of Rooshall, which has disappeared without trace. Thus Sarratt has three areas of settlement, and the large green which is now its centre was not the first, since Church End is on lower ground and closer to the river which was the original source of water. Sarratt's green has a pond and the village pump and is well known in the district for its August fair, which turns the green into a quagmire for a few days if the weather is wet, and for the large bonfire lit on it each 5 November.

The green at Chipperfield, nearby, is part of a large common and has a cricket pitch on it. On one side is the former manor house, on another the village church, and on a third side the school and the Two Brewers inn, where prize-fighters were once trained. Legend has it that the women of Chipperfield once made the mistake of jeering at Richard III when he rode across this green during a stay at Langley Palace. The King took his revenge, it is said, by decreeing that henceforth widows of the parish should not be permitted the dowries from their husbands' estates, as had been the custom.

Close to Rickmansworth, Croxley Green is a long, triangular stretch of green with a well-head and some attractive houses beside it; and at the other side of Watford, Shenley has a smaller green with the village pond and lock-up. The latter is an eighteenth-century circular brick chamber, or cage, with a domed top and small windows with bars in them, and the inscriptions 'Do well, Fear not, Be vigilant, Be sober.'

Nestling below the western beech-clad escarpment of the Chilterns lies Aldbury, which is an epitome of the green villages of England, though to my mind one of the features that make it so famous should long ago have been removed. The village stocks and whipping post, standing beside the large horse-pond on the triangular green, are not quaint relics of rural life but harsh reminders of barbarism defiling an idyllic scene, with old brick and timber-framed cottages, bakehouse and inn surrounding a village centre well known to television viewers.

All signs of the unsavoury communal activities at Gubblecote have fortunately disappeared. Thomas Colley, a local chimney sweep and rabble-rouser, instigated mob violence against an elderly local couple here in 1751, on the grounds that they had bewitched a local farm. John and Ruth Osborn were dragged from the vestry of the church where they had gone to hide, and were stripped naked, tied together and dragged through a pond. They both died from the effects of this ordeal.

tered, Hertfordshire.
tored thatched
tages beside the green
his peaceful and
ractive village.

Colley was convicted of murder and hanged at Wilstone Green, where his body was left in chains on a gibbet, exciting rumours of a black hound that haunted the place afterwards and was believed to be Colley's disembodied spirit.

Leverstock Green is now practically absorbed into Hemel Hempstead, but its triangular green is still there, the flint church of All Saints overlooking it, with a twin bellcote on its roof. Cupid Green is an evocative name now lost within the boundaries of Hemel Hempstead.

Childwick Green and Hatching Green, near Harpenden, are among well-kept greens in the suburban residential southern half of Hertfordshire, the former being a nineteenth-century creation in a model village. Harpenden was itself a pleasant green village until quite recently but is now grown into a small town, with double yellow lines round its greens to prove it. Generally speaking, however, it is the more rural north of the county, well distanced from London, where Hertfordshire remains relatively unspoiled and greens proliferate.

Ayot Green is delightfully open and unspoiled, and quite large for Hertfordshire at over seven acres, with some nice trees on it, whilst the green at Preston, farther north, is tiny but manages to keep trees on it as well as the old village pump. Ayot Green, by the way, has a cottage which was once a toll-house, and it is said that in 1877, when the toll was removed, the occasion was celebrated with free ale for the villagers, who helped themselves from a barrel put on the green by the landlord of the Red Lion.

Westmill, Hertfordshire, triangular green with the village pump.

Ardeley is a characteristically scattered parish of five settlements reached by narrow lanes, with a green almost surrounded by thatched cottages and village hall and having a brick well-head in the middle and the church opposite, beyond a lychgate. A traditional village centre, we might suppose, in this ancient place, once called Yardley, where the first historian of Hertfordshire, Sir Henry Chauncy, was born in 1632. But Ardeley is deceiving us. The green and cottages, and the village hall in matching style, were actually put there only in 1917 by the lord of the manor, to the design of his architect, F. C. Eden.

Benington, on the other hand, has a genuinely ancient and attractive green with all the ingredients that make candidates for the title of 'prettiest village' – duckpond, inn, cottages and, across the road, the church with one of those diminutive local spires known as a 'Hertfordshire spike'. Petronilla de Benstede, the lady of the manor, knew this green in the fourteenth century, for she and her husband lived in the moated castle nearby, and it was she who built the church.

Chauncy tells us that in the fourteenth century a piece of land close to the now-depopulated village of Chesfield, north of Stevenage, was the scene of a dispute over parish boundaries between John Smyth, the vicar of Graveley, and Robert Shorthale, vicar of Chesfield. Christian charity was not much in evidence when valuable tithes were liable to be lost, and the two clerks in holy orders fought for their territorial rights, the reverend Shorthale actually being killed by his fellow clergyman. The land has been known as Parsons Green ever since.

Cottered is a peaceful and spacious place intermingled with nine acres of green, the main part of which is a triangular area at a road junction, and this was undoubtedly the ancient nucleus of an Anglo-Saxon village. The church stands at one side, and opposite is a farmhouse called 'The Lordship', formerly a moated manor house of which fifteenth-century parts survive. This village lay on an old pilgrims' way to the shrine of Our Lady at Walsingham, in Norfolk, and in the church is a fourteenth-century wall painting of St Christopher, patron saint of travellers, with a landscape and figures depicting some of the hazards of such medieval journeying.

Perhaps the most photogenic of all Hertfordshire's village greens is the one at Westmill. It is a triangular green of three quarters of an acre with the village pump at the centre, and the tower of the village church with its 'spike' rising above the roofs of the old cottages on one side, though nowadays television aerials compete with the spire for domination of the skyline. The pump is sheltered from the elements by a tiled conical cap on four timber posts. At the top end of the green stands Westmill

Bury, the brick eighteenth-century manor house. The green also sports a signpost which includes directions to 'Nasty', and in roughly the same direction as that ill-named hamlet is Cherry Green, where Charles Lamb's 'commodious residence', the tiny cottage called Buttonsnap, still stands. Lamb was a great lover of Hertfordshire, where some of his relations lived, and the cottage was the only house he ever owned. He never lived in it, and sold it again after three years.

Braughing (pronounced Braffing) is an ancient settlement reached from the west by a ford across the River Rib, liable to be blocked by the village ducks, but when you get across it, you come to a fine village green graced by old cottages and trees, in what is called 'The Square'. But this is no place to quibble about names. The derivation of the village name is said to be from 'Breahingas' or some such name of a Saxon lord, but it has also been spelt Brakinghe and Brawghing in its time. The green, at any rate, was known to the Saxons if not to the Romans. The place was at an important road crossing in Roman times, and there is a network of ancient green ways throughout this district.

Standon, across the river, is at the junction of the Roman Ermine Street and Stane Street and is not surprisingly a street village, but like so many places in Hertfordshire it has its Green End, and this is associated with a more up-to-date Latin invader than the Roman legions, for in 1784 the balloonist Vincenzo Lunardi landed here after his pioneering flight, causing the local population to flee in panic until a young woman 'who was fritned at first and Run away, thought it the Devill', caught the rope that Lunardi threw to her and helped him to land.

The names of many Hertfordshire greens – some still there, some long gone – attest to the former uses to which they were put or arouse our curiosity about how they were so named. There are Bowman's Green and Bulls Green, Pigs Green and Sandpit Green, Battlers Green, Kettle Green, Tea Green and Flanders Green among the many other corners of this green county for which we have no space. But we will bring our Hertfordshire tour to its conclusion at Great Amwell, where the green is most unusual. Indeed, it may not qualify technically as a village green at all, and it was certainly never the ancient nucleus of the settlement, but it ought to be mentioned here by virtue of that appealing variety it brings, characteristic of the patches of grassland throughout the country, of all shapes and sizes, which are at the hearts of rural communities.

Amwell's green is a well-trimmed lawn on a little island in the so-called New River. It is shaded by weeping willows and bears a stone monument to the New River's creator, Sir Hugh Myddleton, for the 'river' is actually a canal – an artificial waterway constructed in 1613 to carry water from springs at Chadwell and Great Amwell to Clerkenwell, forty miles away, 'conveying', as the monument's inscrip-

Stansted Mountfitchet, Essex. Time for reflection on the green at the centre of this village, near Bishop's Stortford.

tion says, 'health, pleasure and convenience to the metropolis of Great Britain . . .'.

No such beneficial view of things was in mind when Hope End Green, just across the Hertfordshire border in Essex, came by its depressing name, but not far away is the nine-acre Rickling Green, which might itself have changed its name to Hope End Green in 1882 if there had not already been such a place. In that year, the village cricket team saw their opponents knock up a modest little score of 920 runs in response to the home side's 94.

There can be no doubt as to which is the best-known village green in Essex. Finchingfield is one of the most visited and photographed villages in England, and the view up towards the church from the white-fenced pond on the green is in practically every book on village England. The village actually has two greens, but the more famous one near the church is triangular, the other – at the west end of the village – being like a long balloon squeezed tightly in the middle. The houses round the triangular green are of assorted styles, like those at Sarratt. The green is split up by roads, and a bridge crosses the stream that feeds the pond. The inn on the green is the Fox, once an important coaching inn at this meeting place of several old roads. Its front is attractively pargeted – a design feature which would tell us at once, if we did not know, that we were in the eastern counties of England between Thames and Wash.

Finchingfield's reputation as one of the classic villages of England is based on two effects. One is its visual harmony. There are more beautiful village greens than Finchingfield's, more stylish buildings elsewhere and prettier duckponds. But at Finchingfield these various elements have come together in a haphazard but entirely harmonious development which has its appeal in the 'natural' appearance of the place, as opposed to those villages which sometimes look 'planned' even if they were not. If it were not that the green is so patently triangular, it would be impossible to believe that Finchingfield was ever laid out with *any* village plan in mind, much less that of defence. The second effect is more abstruse and in a sense contradicts the first. The English people generally, for all their genuine yearning for rural peace, have a fear of solitude and want – perhaps unconsciously – to be at the centre of things. Finchingfield satisfies this requirement entirely and is thus pleasing psychologically as well as visually, whereas another extremely pretty village, such as Wendens Ambo, does not fulfil the need in such comprehensive fashion.

Weathersfield, just down the road from Finchingfield, also has a triangular green, with the village church and cottages close by, and although it is very attractive, it is more spread out and does not have that peculiar chemistry which makes its neighbour so immensely popular.

Finchingfield's stream is a tributary of the ill-named River Pant which flows through Great Bardfield, where the village square at the meeting of roads was once a green, as was the triangular Falcon Square at Castle Hedingham, with the inn on it. Among other interesting green names of Essex are Molehill Green, Ugley Green, Eight Ash Green and Margaretting Mill Green. East Hanningfield lies along a road south-east of Chelmsford and has a green called 'The Tye', shaped somewhat like a fish, running beside it and looking much the same as it did nearly four hundred years ago, when a cartographer made a map of it in the early seventeenth century. The church here is in ruins beyond the north end of the green. Could the green's name here be an allusion to its tying the community together?

Terling is one of the Essex villages where the green still exists – very wide, with attractive old cottages alongside. Around the eastern side of Braintree, Witham and Feering are good villages round small greens, while at Earls Colne, Pound Green has a Victorian pump on it with an inscription: 'This well was digged . . . in thankful commemoration of the absence of cholera for the common use of the people to pro-

Above: Evenley, Northamptonshire. An unusually formal Midland green with cottages grouped closely round its square perimeter.

Right: Hallaton, Leicestershire. The conical market cross and war memorial occupy parts of this sloping green separated by a pathway.

THE HEARTLAND OF GREEN VILLAGES

voke them to cleanliness.' One detects the hand of a righteous parson in composing that provocative little epistle. Over to the east, Great Bentley has the largest green in Essex – a huge area dwarfing the houses when viewed across it, and accommodating several football pitches in one corner of its forty-five acres. It qualifies as a village green by virtue of having been left to the villagers by a local act in the year of Waterloo.

Stock has a long green running along the middle of its High Street and is uncharacteristic of this part of the country. But at Writtle, right on the fringes of Chelmsford nowadays, is one of the best greens in the county, intact despite the fact that Writtle grew to market town status. It is triangular and has a duckpond on it and some attractive houses around, including Aubyns, a half-timbered and gabled Tudor house, beyond which stands the village church. Because the church is isolated from both the green and the linear extension of the village to the east, it is thought that the green, as well as the street, was developed *after* the establishment of the original village centre, but I do not think that necessarily follows.

At South Benfleet, near Southend, a disturbance was caused on the Sunday before Michaelmas in 1597 by one William Haynes, who was brought before the ecclesiastical court for dancing on the green with minstrels during divine service in the church. No doubt both he and the minstrels were severely reprimanded and forbidden to repeat such a shocking offence on pain of excommunication.

Clavering was mentioned earlier to exemplify a village with more than one green, and other Essex villages have this small scattering of settlements round greens, as – for instance — at Wimbish and Leaden Roding. Henham's central five-acre green is especially attractive, but it is not its only one; there are three others in the parish. Near Thaxted is the hamlet of Cutler's Green, reminding us that the town was at one time an important centre of cutlery manufacture.

Havering-atte-Bower is right on the border of Greater London, within a stone's throw of Romford, but it somehow manages to cling to its rural character, and at its centre is a large green which, not so long ago, was known for its stately elms. The church and some weatherboarded houses stand round it, and the village stocks remain on it near the church. Gallows Green at Aldham reminds us of even worse things, but that is officially designated as common land and not a village green.

Hertfordshire's neighbour on the opposite side from the flat land of Essex is Buckinghamshire, and most of the more attractive greens in this county occur amid or around the gentle slopes of the Chiltern Hills. If they have a greater diversity of size, shape and surroundings than we are accustomed to find in one small area, that may be partly explained by the facts that settlement was relatively late in what a seventh-century monk referred to as the 'deserts of Chiltern', and that no pattern

best-known and most photogenic of all the village greens of East Anglia.

was to be set by arable farming customs in this chalky and heavily wooded region. 'Desert' may seem an odd word to describe hills thick with trees, but it was used in the sense of dry and waterless, for no river or stream penetrated these hills, and although natural springs sufficed for the needs of prehistoric nomads who passed this way, the lack of surface water deterred extensive settlement until relatively recent times. We should expect to find many a village well or pump in the vicinity of the Chiltern village greens, and when we come across a village pond in this region, we can be fairly sure that it is of artificial origin. The chalk soaks up rainfall too rapidly to form natural reservoirs, and the late settlers made ponds by lining pits with clay bonded with straw.

Chenies has neither pond nor pump, being a model village created by the earls of Bedford for the workers on their estates. They resided then at the Tudor manor house to which a path leads from the neat village green, past the church. The village houses were built of red brick round a sloping green in the mid-nineteenth century. The green, however, is triangular and was, no doubt, already there at the centre of an older community when the Russells — whose spectacular monuments in the church's Bedford Chapel are among the treasures of England – elected to rebuild the village on what were then considered modern and generous principles.

The neighbouring village of Latimer is older and more casual than Chenies, although it too was given the 'model village' treatment in Victorian times. But its small green supports not only the parish pump and war memorial but also a rather more unusual feature – the grave of a horse. The lord of the manor, Lord Chesham, commanded a company of the Bucks Hussars in the Boer War, and his life was saved by a French general who was killed in riding between Lord Chesham and his attackers. The general's horse was wounded, and Lord Chesham brought it back to Latimer, burying its heart and harness on the green as a mark of his gratitude.

Tylers Green now seems squeezed in between Penn and High Wycombe but was quite separate from both not so long ago. The green here is actually a twenty-five-acre common, with a large, reed-lined pond where local boys catch tiddlers, but it has the character of a village green, with houses and shops lining it on both sides. The name comes from the makers of the flooring tiles for which Penn was noted in medieval times. The green has a French connection, too, for the philosopher and statesman Edmund Burke, who lived at Beaconsfield, founded a school here for French boys who had been brought to England to escape the Revolution.

Penn itself has four greens, the central one being triangular, with a pond at one of the angles, but the green at Penn Street, a little way to the north, is more interesting. The Chilterns were the chief centre of the chair-making industry, and chair 'bodgers' worked in the beech woods before mechanization made High Wycombe

Tylers Green, Buckinghamshire. The pond, well stocked with reeds, is on common la beside the main road, w the Red Lion among th houses on the opposite side.

the centre of factory furniture. (The bodgers made chair legs for the craftsmen who assembled them.) One old chair factory was the building next door to the inn on the village green at Penn Street. Perhaps the chair-makers came out for their fresh air and exercise to play cricket on the green, and started a tradition here, for the cricket pitch is a well-established village institution, and the inn itself is called 'The Hit or Miss', with a sign showing the early version of the game in progress. The inn doubles as the pavilion for the local team and is a favourite rendezvous for town folk going out for a drink on summer evenings.

Knotty Green and Forty Green are nearby, on the fringes of Beaconsfield, while on the other side of the M40 motorway is Wooburn Green, clasped tight in a fork in the busy roadways but still important as the community's centre and the scene of traditional pastimes on bank holidays. We are near the Thames here, and further upstream is Hambleden, famous for its white bargeboarded old water-mill but having at the village centre a tiny triangular green just big enough for the village pump and a chestnut tree, and with manor house and church accompanying the flint and brick cottages around it. Villagers used this pump to obtain their water until 1956. The churchyard contains the grave of Viscount Hambleden, the Victorian politician and lord of the manor who is rather better known to the general public as the newsagent and bookseller W. H. Smith.

North of Hambleden, secluded in their own little valleys among the beechy slopes, are the tranquil villages of Turville and Fingest, each with its green and Fingest having a cricket pitch beside a buttercup-filled meadow and the Norman church with its well-known twin-saddleback-roofed tower. Turville's green is roughly triangular and has around it as peaceful-looking a group of brick and half-timbered buildings as you could find anywhere, together with the church and Bull and Butcher inn. These hidden villages once provided security for outlaws and highway-men, and even now you can only reach Turville by single-track roads.

Bradenham, on the other hand, has a big-open green by the roadside that is irresistibly inviting on hot summer afternoons when there is nothing better to do than laze about on the grass. This green brings to mind an anonymous rustic verse:

> As I was laying on the green,
> A little book it chanced I seen.
> Carlyle's *Essay on Burns* was the edition –
> I left it laying in the same position.

Any real interest in literature here may well have been confined at one time to the brick manor house which stands a few yards from the flint church overlooking the green on the east side. It is an elegant seventeenth-century house and was the home of Isaac d'Israeli, the antiquary and father of the Prime Minister, whose education began in his father's library in this house. Isaac himself was educated at Leiden University and wrote numerous books, his *Curiosities of Literature* being the best known. He was called 'the king of all the bookworms'. Stone pillars at the side of the green mark a straight path across it to the manor house gates, and the village, which is now in the protection of the National Trust, features in Benjamin Disraeli's novel *Endymion*. The statesman retained his love for the Chilterns throughout his life.

Skittle Green, Lacey Green, Chambersgreen and Stony Green are among the interesting names of other Chiltern greens, while secluded hill villages with peaceful greens include Radnage, Asheridge and Jordans, the last two associated with Aneurin Bevan and William Penn the Quaker, respectively.

Buckinghamshire beyond the Chilterns has no better village green to boast than that at Haddenham, between Aylesbury and Thame. It is a widely scattered village with a stream running through it from Town's End in the north to Church End

oburn Green,
kinghamshire. Bank
day pastime on the
ngular green at this
age near Beaconsfield.

at the southern extremity. Its antiquity is evidenced by some of the local names for lanes and areas of the village, such as Dragontail, Dollicot, Fort End and Skittles Green, and the names of plots of land associated with the medieval open field system of farming have been recorded, to say nothing of a villager whose memorial is in the church and was named Gylls Wodbryge. The main green at Church End is a fairly large, unspoiled patch of grassland of irregular shape surrounded by houses, barns, school and church. There is a duckpond at one corner which laps the church-yard wall, and as the church tower is a tall, arcaded Early English affair with square top, the scene is momentarily reminiscent of Venice, but the impression is instantly dispelled by the thatched roofs and the house walls round it, for the latter are of

93

ville, Buckingham-
re. One of the county's
ghtful Chiltern
ages, with brick and
ber cottages accom-
ying the Bull and
cher inn round the
all green.

witchert, a local speciality consisting of chalk marl mixed with straw and water, which made serviceable walls provided they were, like Devon cob, given a stone base and a good covering of thatch. The ducks on the village pond here are the successors of those which provided the foundation of the Aylesbury duck-breeding business which long supplied birds to be eaten with green peas at tables throughout the land and beyond. There used to be a Duck Street, where the early breeders lived. This muddy village pond ought to be holy water to the gourmet.

Cuddington and Westlington, near by, both have small greens with witchert houses round them. Cuddington's is divided into Upper Green and Lower Green, and the parish pump survives at the top end. Its neighbour to the north, Lower or Nether Winchendon, has a fine little green at the centre of the village, with the church and some nice old cottages gathered round it. Some of these are of witchert, too, but the curiosity here is a Victorian pillarbox of stone with a ball finial on top.

The Vale of Aylesbury is dotted with remote villages reached by long drives along country roads, and the one we should head for in the present context is Quainton. Its $1\frac{1}{2}$-acre green is roughly triangular and is on a steep slope, with all its interest at the top end. It is dominated by a brick-built tower mill, built in 1832, formerly derelict but partly restored by local volunteers since. It stands high above the village, with three old cottages at its foot which were converted into one fine modern home.

ldenham, Bucking-
nshire. The green at
rch End is a traditional
al centre, but the well-
wn duckpond had
d up when this
tograph was taken
ing the drought of
84.

Near this house on the green itself are the pedestal and broken shaft of the fifteenth-century market cross, round which itinerant traders would have gathered in medieval times and from where, no doubt, proclamations would have been 'broadcast' to the community by the parish beadle. There are houses down both sides of the green, one of which is called 'Magpie', the cottage where George Lipscomb was born, son of the sailor and surgeon James Lipscomb. George lived here for many years, devoting himself almost heroically to writing an eight-volume history of Buckinghamshire, and dying a pauper with the ink still almost wet on his last page of manuscript.

Right over on the county's eastern border, Edlesborough has a small green over which the noted village church, perched on its lofty hill, watches like an eagle. Thornborough, to the north, retains its village stocks as well as a pond and some picturesque cottages around small pieces of green. Other small greens at this end of Buckinghamshire occur at such as Soulbury and Castlethorpe.

V

Central Southern England

HAMPSHIRE, WILTSHIRE, BERKSHIRE
AND OXFORDSHIRE

The numerous village greens of Hampshire are often distinguished by their considerable size. The village of Hartley Wintney, in the county's north-east corner, seems to have possessed at least eleven greens at one time, as well as the twenty-three-acre common and the sixty-five-acre common at Phoenix Green. Common rights are attached to one or two of Hartley Wintney's surviving greens, which are mostly heavily wooded, though there is a small duckpond beside the busy main road through this large village. But the one that introduces us to the characteristic Hampshire green is Cricketers Green, for the county that boasts the one-time home of the famous Hambledon Club at Broadhalfpenny Down is still devoted to the village game.

Yet Hambledon itself is a street village, and when we think of Hampshire's villages and hamlets, it is far from automatic to visualize a green at the centre of a community. We are more likely to think of fast-flowing trout streams, trickling brooks and little bridges, with water-mills here and there and willows along the banks, from which fine cricket bats have long been made. In fact, Hampshire's villages are often set among rough pastures and large, open commons which we shall not easily confuse as the centres of local settlements. Most of the county's greens are in its eastern half, and for no clearly discernible reason the River Test seems to form the boundary in this region between the area where village greens occur frequently and that where they do not. Wiltshire, to the west, has relatively few greens; Berkshire hardly any at all.

Eversley is another village at the north-eastern edge of Hampshire which has a green complete with cricket pitch, and it was well known to Charles Kingsley, who was rector here and wrote *The Water Babies* in the rectory. He was buried in the churchyard.

Hambledon has only one rival as Hampshire's most famous village world-wide, and that is Selborne. Gilbert White's village has a green known as 'the Plestor', and beyond an ancient yew, much praised by White, is the churchyard where the parson-naturalist is buried. Cobbett came here in 1823 – thirty years after White's death – and measured the yew's girth at twenty-three feet eight inches. The Plestor is a small, well-kept, sloping piece of ground which was granted as a market-place in the thirteenth century by the lord of the manor, Adam de Gurdon. Gilbert White's house, 'Wakes', was on the west side of the green, and it is now a museum devoted to White and to Captain L. E. G. Oates, who died with Scott in Antarctica.

Preston Candover is the largest and most northerly of the three Candover villages stretched out along the Alresford–Basingstoke road, and though its very situation marks it as a street village, it once had a sizeable green on which stood the village pump along with a pond and a livestock pound. The green has shrunk to a small triangle of land, but the pump is still on it, accompanied by a war memorial.

Old and New Alresford are separated only by the river from which they take their names, and New Alresford was, in any case, only *new* in the thirteenth century. It had five cricket greens once. No wonder Mary Russell Mitford said that Hampshire is the Greece of cricket and Alresford its Athens. What could be more appropriate than that it should have been, more recently, the home of one of the game's modern prophets, John Arlott. But cricket subsequently moved across the river to Old Alresford, where the long, triangular green has weeping willows beside the stream.

There are those who regard village cricket as a joke in these days of the high-powered professional and high-financed international game, but I am not among them. We may still smile at the old images of the local match on the village green. The stories of Sundays when villagers went to church in their white flannels, and the rector had his own on under his surplice, ready for play immediately after the benediction, still amuse us, because the air of enthusiasm and compromise is so much a part of our English character. We are as much tickled as foreigners are by our own eccentricity, when we read of the hymn board being brought out of church to serve another purpose: the figures that an hour before had told the congregation in their pews that the next hymn was number 129 now informing the spectators in their deckchairs that the home side are nineteen for two wickets. But the days when scythes cut the grass on the pitch and sheep cropped the outfield, and the village blacksmith thundered down the slope in his braces to bowl the first ball, are over. The modern village game is taken seriously, and every side wants to get to Lords and win the Whitbread Village Trophy.

This serious approach to the game inevitably means that village greens are being abandoned in favour of bigger and better playing fields donated by the squire or rented from the farmer; and the appealing air of compromise and informality about the game played on a green that is barely large enough, and where you score six if you hit the ball into the duckpond, is gradually being lost.

Village cricket has made an appearance in the works of Charles Dickens, George Meredith, H. G. Wells and J. M. Barrie, as well as Mary Russell Mitford and, of course, Hugh de Selincourt and A. G. Macdonnell. But perhaps the most appropriate literary reference in the present context is R. C. Sherriff's play *Badger's Green*, first produced in 1930 and subsequently filmed. The story concerns a fictitious Hampshire village called Badger's Green, to which a property developer comes intent on turning the village into a profitable leisure complex, until he is won over by the charm of a cricket match in which, pressed into service, he scores the winning run, whereupon he becomes vice-president of the club and decides to build elsewhere. Such sentimental pleasantries are hardly likely to impress hard-headed capitalists today, and the dangers are real enough, but I suppose we may rest assured that Hampshire, at any rate, will be among the last counties to give up those village greens on which their weekend cricket matches are played.

Cheriton and Kilmeston – not far apart, to the east of Winchester – are both attractive villages with greens at their centres, though Cobbett, riding from one to the

Hartley Wintney, Hampshire. The fine pavilion on Cricketers Green, complete with clock, scoreboard, flagpole, seats and, of course, empty beer cask

other, had little to say for either. He called Cheriton 'a little, hard, iron village', and Kilmeston 'now mouldered into two farms, and a few miserable tumble-down houses for the labourers'. But he did not miss Kilmeston's manor house, the large brick mansion which the Prince Regent lived in for a time. The green itself, alas, is now no more than a rough area of grass disfigured by signs, bus shelter and pillarbox, the scars of urban fever.

Cheriton's green has the pub which lays claim to the shortest pub name in the country – the H.H. – but as this is only an abbreviation of Hampshire Hunt, I suppose it must be disqualified on that account. It stands at the end of an elongated triangle. A stream runs through the green with little bridges crossing it to reach the houses on the far side.

Near the West Sussex border is Buriton, well known as the birthplace of the historian Edward Gibbon, and it has a green of sorts even if it is nearly all taken up by the village pond. A little farther south is Chalton, where the rambling green is flanked by church and pub, both ancient. The Red Lion is a timber-framed building with a thatched roof, dating from the sixteenth century or possibly earlier. Stubbington is the 'green' half of Crofton-and-Stubbington on the Gosport peninsula.

The village greens of West Hampshire occur mainly in and around the New Forest,

...orne, Hampshire. The ...rming little green ...de famous by the ...teenth-century ...son-naturalist Gilbert ...ite.

Old Alresford, Hampsh[ire]. Splendid willows borde[r] the stream passing through this triangula[r] green in the village wh[ose] name is pronounced 'Allsford'.

Cheriton, Hampshire. T[he] stream through the gre[en] looks more like a miniature canal, but its only traffic is a flotilla o[f] ducks, and they don't mind.

and the forest's famous capital, Lyndhurst, is at the centre of several villages and hamlets whose greens, not surprisingly, are subject to common rights. The greens at Cadnam and Swan Green are especially notable, Cadnam's being in the ownership of the National Trust.

Bramshaw is a scattered parish with a green at Nomansland which has a cricket pitch where the batsman may hit a six in Hampshire and be run out in Wiltshire. But Woodgreen and Breamore are more characteristic of these parts, with unfenced greens around the villages, instead of at their centres, and open to New Forest ponies which wander in to graze among the oak trees. Minstead, that delightfully quiet village where Sir Arthur Conan Doyle is buried in the churchyard, is likewise a typical forest clearing with houses joining the village shop and the aforementioned Trusty Servant Inn round its little green.

At Hampshire's western extremity is Martin, where the green sports the parish pump and must have contributed to the village being four times runner-up in the county's 'best-kept village' competition, until it finally won the coveted title itself a few years ago. The green has neat thatched cottages round it, and council building policy has prevented the intrusion of hideous modern houses which would have deprived Martin of its honour.

Pamber Green and Turgis Green are among the green village names of Hampshire where the greens themselves have disappeared, but Beggars Green and Spanish Green are still there – the latter at Hartley Wespall – and the name of Bears Green at Winchfield speaks for itself.

The Isle of Wight is not famed for its village greens – Keats Green at Shanklin, with its gorgeous display of hydrangeas, is not a village green in any sense. But Calbourne has a triangular green with the church at one corner. There is also a green at Chale.

We may pass into Wiltshire at this point, for although village greens are fairly thin on the ground in this county of chalk, a few green villages here are especially worthy of notice. Alderbury is the first worth noticing as we cross the border in the south-east corner near Salisbury. It has a triangular green with the pub, the Green Dragon, beside it, on which Dickens based his 'Blue Dragon' in *Martin Chuzzlewit*, for he was then staying near the village at the former home of the young architect Pugin.

Wilton has a formal green in its Kingsbury Square, with several nice Georgian houses round it, but Wilton is not a village and has not been for a long time, being one of the oldest boroughs in England, so we may assume this green to be a relatively modern creation; and as if there were not enough Winterbornes or Winterbournes in Dorset – fourteen in all – we find half a dozen villages with this prefix in Wiltshire.

Minstead, Hampshire. A characteristic New Forest village green, where ponies enjoy the facilities as well as human visitors

The name occurs on chalk lands and denotes a stream which dries up in summer, as the water soaks through the surface. But though the Winterbornes are in the eastern half of the county, none of them has a notable green.

Right across in the south-west corner is Stourton, famous only by association, since it is the village from which one enters the magnificent Stourhead Gardens, laid out in the mid-eighteenth century for Henry Hoare. But there is a village green near the church, and on a mound nearby stands the High Cross, a splendid Gothic monument which originally belonged to Bristol and was brought here in 1765. Its lower part dates from the fourteenth century and bears statues of medieval kings, while the upper part was a Stuart addition with four more monarchs, culminating with Charles I.

Not far away is Zeals, where a war memorial in the form of a limestone cross stands on a stepped base and lists the names of villagers who lost their lives in the 1914–18 war. There are some nice trees on the green, with one or two attractive houses grouped loosely around.

A few miles to the north is Horningsham, near Longleat, and though Pevsner calls it a 'singularly loose village' with 'no visual cohesion', it has a pleasant enough green as its nucleus, sloping and triangular, with the village pub beside it, dutifully called the Bath Arms.

Steeple Ashton has a wide open area at the village centre known as 'The Green', with some nice houses round it, but the actual grass there has shrunk somewhat to a small patch with the village cross and lock-up and some strips or verges in front of the houses. The lock-up is an octagonal stone building with a domed roof, and you would think from the outside that the local drunks and felons thrown in there for the night were being treated to a style to which they were not accustomed.

Urchfont is not far away, and it has a green and a large duckpond at its centre. This is, to my mind, one of the most beautiful and satisfying of village centres, and although the pond occupies a large proportion of the green on one side, there is still an attractive area of grass amid the stylish brick houses and lovely trees which make Urchfont's nucleus one to cherish. The pond is fed by the spring which, according to the experts, gives the place its name, from 'Eohric's fount'. Behind the green is the village church of St Michael, with its fine fourteenth-century chancel. Poulshot's church, on the other hand, is a mile away from the large green there, which has the main road running through the middle of it.

Farther north on the Cotswold fringes is Biddestone, with a long, stylish green terminated by the duckpond and flanked by fine houses of grey stone, roofed with stone tiles. One of them has a gazebo in the garden wall, where travellers waiting for the arrival of the coach at the nearby inn were wont to take shelter from rain or sun.

Castle Eaton, up in the north by Cricklade, has the Red Lion beside its green, the inn being built of brick whereas much of the village centre is of grey limestone. The village stands on the bank of the stripling River Thames.

The stream which gave Aldbourne, on the Marlborough Downs near the Berkshire border, its name, feeds the Kennet. As you come into this attractive village from the Hungerford side, the road bends round a disappointing part of the village green with a rather pathetic-looking round pond full of litter (notwithstanding the nearby litter bins). But a narrow lane links this with the larger green sloping upward, with houses and cottages either side and the church at the top – a classic English village scene. There is an ancient cross on the green where men who made bells here once took the air, and the one-time prosperity of their foundry explains some of the stylish houses round the green. Most of the older bells in Wiltshire churches came from this village, where the trade flourished for two centuries up to 1826.

Among other Wiltshire villages with greens – mostly small triangular ones – are Burbage, Everleigh and Collingbourne Ducis.

Berkshire has its full share of attractive villages, but we associate them either with the open downland or with the banks of the Thames, and some of the green villages the county *did* once possess have been lost to Oxfordshire, like Sutton Courtenay, for example, where the ancient church stands set back from the good sized triangular green, and among the tree-shaded graves in the churchyard are those of George Orwell and Prime Minister Asquith. The Swan and the George and Dragon are rival inns on this green. Arborfield has a small triangular green at the roadside, just big enough for a seat and the war memorial cross.

'Green' names abound in the north-east corner of Berkshire. Cox Green, Kiln Green, Littlewick Green, Burchetts Green, Pinkney's Green and Cockpole Green are all near Maidenhead, Pinkney's Green being a large common owned by the National Trust. But the famous one here is at Cookham, on account of its association with

Sutton Courtenay, Oxfordshire. Formerly Berkshire, this village's pleasant triangular green has both the Swan and George and Dragon for company.

the artist Sir Stanley Spencer. Of course, it is the river-side scene which gives the village its reputation as a beauty spot, but the green is lined with attractive houses, and no doubt the village's most eccentric resident used to be seen crossing it now and then with his old pram full of paints, brushes and canvas. Various parts of Cookham are in his paintings, some of which are religious, some erotic, and some religious *and* erotic, such as his *Village in Heaven*, which features the phallic war memorial on the so-called Cookham Moor. The neighbouring Cookham Dean also has a small green.

Greenham Common has no particular relevance in our present context, but it is very hard to ignore nowadays, as a one-time part of this green and pleasant land now turned to base uses. Skinners Green – less celebrated or reviled – is also near Newbury. Aldworth, high up on the Berkshire Downs, has a tiny green dominated by the village well, which is nearly four hundred feet deep beneath its elaborate timbers and clanky machinery. The Bell Inn stands opposite.

Steventon, Baulking, Goosey and Stanford-in-the-Vale are among the green villages which Oxfordshire acquired from Berkshire in the local government reorganization of the seventies. Steventon's green is a generous long one from which the Causeway, an elevated cobbled path lined with trees, leads to the church a considerable distance away. There can hardly be any doubt in this case that the green came before the church; the villagers would hardly go to the lengths of building a dry causeway from the old church to the new green.

Baulking's large, unkempt green is subject to common rights, and Goosey's, also large, is picturesque when the buttercups are in flower amid scattered small stone cottages. The village church is at one end. Its name seems to mean Goose Island, the settlement having once been stranded in the marshy valley of the River Ock, from which Baulking's name is in turn derived. The inn at Goosey is 'The Pound'.

West Hanney is a village whose green ought to be better cared for. It is a small, triangular area with the manor house close by and one or two cottages and farm buildings around, but the green itself, besides its war memorial cross, is littered with too many road signs, crisp packets and empty cans to qualify as one of the most attractive that Oxfordshire won from Berkshire.

Little Wittenham is another place which Berkshire lost to its expansive neighbour. It has a small green with a First World War memorial on it, bearing only one man's name. But Little Wittenham is only a tiny hamlet, and the one man who lost his life in the war may have been the only one who went to the front. Shrivenham was also in Berkshire a few years ago. It has a pleasant small green with a stone-built Memorial Hall beside it.

When we turn to the old county of Oxfordshire, we find plenty of village greens, but they do not occur so much on the chalk of the Chilterns at the south-east corner, nor in the vale below the hills – though Marsh Baldon and Great Milton are notable exceptions – but chiefly to the north of Oxford, in the Cotswolds and the so-called Redlands.

One of the exceptions in the Chilterns is at Stoke Row, where the $1\frac{1}{2}$-acre green is not especially attractive but reminds us of the water problems in these hills that we first noticed in Buckinghamshire, for nearby is one of the strangest curiosities of village England, an oriental well-head with domed cupola and a cast-iron elephant above the winding gear. It was given to the village by the Maharajah of Benares, who paid for the digging of the well when told by Edward Reade of nearby Ipsden, who was Governor of India's North West Provinces, of the problems the village had in getting its water supply. The well is 368 feet deep and was completed in 1864.

Another Chiltern green occurs at Checkendon, where a wooden seat and a church noticeboard have their backs to the hedge which separates the green from the churchyard. The Norman church is built of flint and has an unusual rounded apse and the largest collection of brasses in the county.

We ought not to pass Marsh Baldon too quickly, for it has a very large and exceptionally interesting green. It was originally a square area, alongside the village street stretching north from the church, and had houses all round it but was liable to flooding – hence the village name. The marsh may have saved the green from being

Baulking, Oxfordshire. This eight-acre green is subject to common rights and has only a few isolated houses and farm buildings round it.

built over. The access points had gates so that the green, which is subject to common rights, could be closed off, and this was done especially when the village's crop of hay was growing, giving rise to many years of dispute over the rights to the green's use. In the eighteenth century there was a sort of running battle between the lady of the manor and a landowner who tried to assert his own rights over the green. The lady had trenches dug and trees planted to prevent the landowner having his way.

Some houses have encroached on the green in one corner, so that its square plan is no longer quite so obvious, but cricket is played on it nowadays, and the annual village fair is held there by long custom. The lane along the east side of the green, known as Blackberry Lane, is on the line of the Roman road between Dorchester and Oxford. Most interesting of all, perhaps, is the fact that the formal shape of the original green was entirely surrounded by houses facing inwards like the supposedly 'defensive' greens of the north of England.

Does it not seem very likely, on the face of it, that the majority of sizeable greens all over the country were originally planned to provide enclosed grazing for livestock, where they could not wander away at night, and that fewer of these greens are left in their original state in the ever-restless south than in the slower-changing north of England?

The old village of Newnham, nearby, was done away with not to provide pasture but to make way for the mansion and park of Lord Harcourt, who built a new village, re-named Nuneham Courtenay, out of sight a mile away. The original green village was replaced by a street village of semi-detached brick houses in the 1760s, and the destruction of the old Newnham is generally thought to have inspired Goldsmith's famous poem 'The Deserted Village':

> Sweet smiling village, loveliest of the lawn,
> Thy sports are fled, and all thy charms withdrawn;
> Amidst thy bowers the tyrant's hand is seen,
> And desolation saddens all the green.

o views of Marsh
don, Oxfordshire. One
he most interesting
ens of central southern
gland, it has similarities
the 'defensive' greens of
north.

The name of Wood Eaton gives a clue to the origin of villages on the clay land north of Oxford, which were clearings in the thick forest when settlement first began. There was a Romano–British settlement a little nearer to the waste land of Otmoor, to the east (which was the scene, once again, of much fierce dispute in the nineteenth century over the enclosure of common land, when villagers pulled down fences). The village green is still at the centre of the Wood Eaton community, supporting a cross erected in the thirteenth century and now despoiled of its head, only the base and shaft remaining. There is also a pond, and the village's elm trees used to be commented on favourably, but these have of course succumbed to the fatal epidemic.

One would expect Ducklington to be furnished with a well-populated village pond, and indeed both pond and green are there, but the origin of the name has nothing to do with ducks, according to those spoil-sport experts on place-names, who explain that it comes from one of those hypothetical Saxons they dream up to explain so many otherwise incomprehensible village names. The name of this Saxon lord was Ducca, so they say.

Bletchingdon and Weston-on-the-Green are friendly neighbours a little way north. Bletchingdon's open fields and surrounding land had already been enclosed, after some riots and legal wrangling, long before the battles of Otmoor took place, but the village green survived and has stone-built cottages along one side. Weston still keeps its stocks on the green.

Over to the west is Hailey, a village divided into separate settlements like so many

of those we noticed in Hertfordshire. Delly End has the main green, a triangular one with a domed war memorial and a row of seventeenth-century terraced cottages facing the manor house across it.

North Leigh is only a stone's throw away, and it is an ancient settlement, with Roman remains in the vicinity, a Saxon tower in its church and much folklore clinging to it like a mist in the valley. The Devil had a peculiar hold on the imagination of the villagers once: Old Nick stumped a group of boys playing cricket on the green by vanishing into thin air after impressing them with his skill. And the village had several ghosts, among them Lady Tanfield's, she being the hated wife of a lord of the manor. With all this superstition, it comes as no great surprise to find that the village had what used to be called the Ducking Stool Pond, where women suspected of witchcraft may once have been 'swum' to test their allegiance to the Devil – a treatment subsequently toned down as an unpleasant punishment for malicious gossips. Happily, this pond where women probably died from drowning or shock was filled in years ago, but unhappily, the green itself has shrunk to a fraction of its former size.

Leafield is another settlement which originated as a clearing in the forest of Wychwood, and an ancient mound known as Leafield Barrow is a prominent landmark nearby. The small green and duckpond here are unlikely to have been at the communal centre of the settlement, but as building went on round it, the green evolved as a village nucleus. In the Middle Ages Leafield folk were regarded by neighbouring villagers as 'strange' or 'foreign', with an uncouth dialect and dark complexion, and one supposes they were an imported community at some stage, perhaps of Celtic rather than Anglo-Saxon origin.

We are in the Oxfordshire Cotswolds now, and we find stylish buildings of stone round the green at Westwell, nestling in a little dip which is a natural for a duckpond, this one being graced by yellow irises and moorhens. The green also bears the war memorial – a monolith on a stepped base – and has the church on rising ground above it, with rectory, manor house, cottages and barns nearby. As with so many of the Cotswold villages, Westwell had its own quarry once and was noted for its stone tiles, which can be seen here roofing the cottages.

Near the corner of Oxfordshire where it joins Gloucestershire and Warwickshire, Cornwell also sits in a hollow, but rather more self-consciously than Westwell. Cornwell was largely rebuilt as a model village in the late 1930s by Clough Williams-Ellis, when he was already rehearsing his special line in picturesque architectural fantasies at Portmeirion. Cornwell is distinctive without being so totally foreign to its surroundings as its builder's more famous creation in Wales, but it looks a bit old-fashioned, like a stage setting for a thirties drawing-room comedy brought out for use in a new play. The green is surrounded by low stone walls ending with piers and ball finials, and the cottages climb up the slopes from the little stream running through the village.

Great Tew is among Oxfordshire's best-known villages, and it too was a model village, built long before Williams-Ellis's time. It was laid out by the young J. C. Loudon, early in the nineteenth century, for the lord of the manor, General Stratton, who was persuaded not to do the usual thing, which was to demolish the unsightly village and build a new one out of sight of the big house. Instead, Loudon designed Great Tew to look picturesque, and did so with great success. The village school is on the green, which is faced by a row of brown ironstone cottages and post office/ store, all with pretty, hedged front gardens and thatched roofs, and nearby is the village pub, the Falkland Arms – not a recent eruption of village jingoism, Lord Falkland having been a lord of the manor in the seventeenth century. Though its prettiness is contrived, Great Tew is worthy of its distinction as an Outstanding

eat Tew, Oxfordshire. A
st attractive village
ntre, but not quite the
cient nucleus it appears,
ving been rebuilt in the
eteenth century.

Conservation Area: it was sad to see such a place falling into the neglected state in which I first encountered it some years ago. As part of its programme of restoration it has removed the stocks which every guidebook says are on the village green.

North Aston has a large triangular green near the point where the road from Great Tew meets that from Middle and Steeple Aston, and Shenington's green with the church on it is at the centre of a stone village where the building material takes on a positively orange colour from the iron oxide in the quarried stone.

Oxfordshire and the Cotswolds have revived their associations with Morris dancers, those dedicated performers of ritual fertility routines on May Day, at Whitsun and on other holidays. The dances performed nowadays are modern substitutes for folk dances and ritual drama of ancient origin which often took place in churchyards, the beribboned hanky-waving men in white with bells on their legs moving from place to place giving their performances of a pagan ceremony which, like the maypole, was fiercely condemned by the Puritans. Philip Stubbes, that zealous defender of Christian morality, attacked the Morris dancers for spending the whole week of Whitsun, as he saw it, in 'drunkennesse, whordome, gluttonie, and other filthie Sodomiticall exercyses'. The Adderbury team of Morris men would hardly subscribe to that view of their harmless activities today, notwithstanding that their village has a history of ribald and sometimes aggressive rivalry with its neighbour, Bloxham; that every encouragement is given to pagan practices by the stone carvings on the cornices of the church; and that the village was the home of the profligate Earl of Rochester, whose house faced the fairly large triangular green.

Adderbury is a spreading toffee-coloured village divided into east and west parts by the Sor brook, and each half has its own green, but East Adderbury's is the most appealing, with several stylish houses around it and the ironstone church – one of the finest in Oxfordshire – close by. The half-acre green, like the Morris men, is at the centre of much pagan imagery and some rum goings-on, for the carvings on the church include mermaids and minstrels with pipes, while a brass inside declares that one Jane Smith, who died in 1508, departed this life on 30 February.

Surviving names like Whiteoak Green, Cookley Green and Christmas Common complete a picture of Oxfordshire, which, for all its industry and urban development, still has a great deal of rural beauty and has retained a fair proportion of its ancient village greens.

VI

The East Midlands and East Anglia

BEDFORDSHIRE, NORTHAMPTONSHIRE, LEICESTERSHIRE, CAMBRIDGESHIRE, SUFFOLK AND NORFOLK, LINCOLNSHIRE AND NOTTINGHAMSHIRE

Moving north from the Home Counties, we find a curious gap in that wealth of village greens up the eastern side of the country. There are greens here, sure enough, but it is not only in the fens where greens seem conspicuous by their absence, for after the profusion of green villages in the south east, the counties in and around East Anglia are distinctly short of greens. The reasons may be related partly to the settlement patterns of the Danes who colonized the region and to the fact that there are large numbers of deserted medieval villages in this area where old settlements were replaced by new linear villages in more hospitable and profitable sites, when there was less need of central open spaces for communal use. There are also many large villages and small towns with triangular market-places which may have been greens originally, and encroachment on greens by squatters has also led to the eventual elimination of greens in many places.

We do not (or should not) expect to find stylish villages in Bedfordshire, but there are a few greens which should not go unnoticed. At the southernmost fringe of the county are the neighbouring villages of Whipsnade and Studham. The greens in both these places are in fact commons, but they masquerade as village greens, with the local shops at their fringes, and most visitors to the zoological gardens cross the one at Whipsnade, standing up on the chalk downs near Dunstable, while Studham's rough green is at the highest point in the county.

Perilously close to Bedford now is Elstow, where John Bunyan was born, and along with the old Moot Hall (now a museum) on the green is the village church where the young Bunyan rang the bells in the detached tower. It was on the green itself, however, that Bunyan claimed to have had his first vision, whilst joining in local revelries on the Sabbath. No doubt it was his conscience that spoke to him, but it turned him on the road to Nonconformist preaching and the creation of one of the greatest allegorical works in the English language, *The Pilgrim's Progress.*

Cardington is not far away and is most famous for its association with airships but ought to be remembered in connection with humanitarian movements far more important to the process of civilization. It was in the second half of the seventeenth century that Bunyan spent his periods in Bedford Gaol, and almost exactly a hundred years later that John Howard of Cardington went there as Sheriff of Bedfordshire and was so shocked by what he found that he set out on *his* great work, the reform of prison conditions. Howard was also a philanthropist who competed with his friend the brewer Samuel Whitbread in housing improvements, and he re-planned the green at Cardington and built cottages and almshouses round it, along with his own brick house. The green used to be graced by stately elm trees, but of course they have succumbed to the wretched beetle.

Houses of similar date to Cardington's surround Ickwell's huge green, a giant of thirteen acres at the centre of what is no more than a hamlet sometimes called Ickwell Green, for there is little else – not even a pub. But the green supports a permanent maypole and a cricket pitch with a thatched pavilion at the side, and one of the buildings round the edge of the green has been in its time the village smithy and the workshop of Ickwell's most famous son, Thomas Tompion, sometimes known as 'the father of English watchmaking' for his invention of the 'dead-beat escapement'.

Harrold's mere half-acre green seems totally insignificant by comparison with Ickwell's, but this village on the Ouse sports a green which is of more than passing interest despite its smallness. The green is lined with trees and has on it the old village lock-up, a circular stone building with a conical roof and large enough to hold more than the odd local drunk whom most such buildings seem to have been designed for. More interesting, however, is the old octagonal market house of timber, which is a symbol of the village's later *raison d'être.* The village was one of those which developed a flourishing cottage industry in lace-making before the Industrial Revolution; the villagers used to go to the green, where the work was distributed among them, and then take the finished lace back to the market house, where it was paid for by the employers. But the rise of factory industry put an end to this local occupation, and the lace-makers had to go to Bedford to work in the factories there.

Harrold, Bedfordshire. eighteenth-century lace market on the green, w the village lock-up visib through the trees in the distance.

Potton and Houghton Regis are other Bedfordshire villages with sizeable greens, but both here and in Northamptonshire the number of greens is small in relation to the number of villages. Northamptonshire is curiously lacking in common land, too, and both facts seem to be related to encroachment and enclosure of land in

the lowland areas of the county. Most of Northamptonshire's greens are in the south-west corner on the limestone belt – a curious contradiction of the general pattern of village green distribution in the country as a whole.

Evenley is close to the Oxfordshire border and has a square green with cottages set neatly round three sides. They are built of limestone and help to give this fine village centre a picturesque quality which makes it one of the best village greens in the whole of the Midlands area. There is a cricket pitch in the middle, and some fine trees round its fringes, although there are two or three stumps of large trees which have had to be cut down. One of them has a plaque on it recording the care Councillor Leonard Warren and his wife Lesley took over all the trees in this attractive village.

It is interesting to note here that, whilst the houses and the village shop and

: King's Sutton,
rthamptonshire. There
nore than one green in
village, but the
;inal centre, called 'The
;are', is in the shadows
he fine church steeple.

post office face the green and almost surround it like the supposedly defensive villages of the north, the access road to them is at their fronts, i.e. it goes between the green and the house fronts, whereas at places like Milburn the original road went round the backs of the buildings, with the green coming right up to the front gates of the houses. I would guess that the green here was of considerably later development than those where the 'defensive' layout is still 'evident'.

King's Sutton, celebrated for its fine church spire, is less formal and has the old stocks on its main green, in 'The Square', with the church and the gabled Jacobean manor house among its surrounding buildings. The stocks have iron railings to protect them from the vandals whom they would have held captive a century or two ago, and stand beside the garden wall of the Bell Inn. There must have been much rumour and gossip in the air above this green early in the seventeenth century, for the vicar was evidently unpopular with some of the community. One married couple was brought before the ecclesiastical court for bidding the minister 'kisse his horse under the taile' and calling him a reprobate and a bloodsucker. The woman, whose name was Denise, had thrown stones at him, hitting him in the face and drawing blood. No wonder her name was mis-spelt 'Dionyse' in the church records! But this couple was not alone in giving the minister a hard time. The local folk threatened him, saying they would ride him out of town if he joined in persecuting the village wise woman, whose ministrations they obviously preferred to his.

Abthorpe has a rectangular green with the village church on it. The Scandinavian name-ending may be misleading. The settlement was probably here already and

ht: The village stocks at
g's Sutton.

was only re-named by the Danes who would have developed the village without changing the existing plan to any great extent.

Moreton Pinkney has a winding road running through it which is said to have been made like this to weave between squatters' cottages which had been built on the green. If so, the more substantial houses subsequently built on the sites of these places have left the village street flanked by wide verges rather than the central green which it must originally have had.

Badby's green is itself irregular, sloping down from the church between stone cottages and having the former village school at its centre. Although Badby's green is split up by roads and paths and ruined by telegraph wires and poles, the village has been regarded in its time as one of the prettiest in the county, and one wonders if it gave pleasure to John Merrick, who must have seen it when he came to Fawsley Park as the guest of the courageous Lady Knightley. He was the grotesquely deformed 'Elephant Man', and a sensitive fellow for all his hideous aspect.

Newnham, nearby, has an area of green also split up by roads, with several trees and signposts and a bus shelter beside the Daventry road, with the village pub, the Romer Arms, overlooking it; and Byfield is a main-road village in the ironstone country graced by a pleasant little sloping green with the stump of an old cross on it.

One of the most fascinating of Northamptonshire's greens, historically speaking, is on higher ground near the county boundary. Hellidon is an interesting village on the Warwickshire border where two greens of irregular shape resulted from haphazard development around a curious knot of minor roads. The more northerly green must always have been the main part, for it had a well at one side and a pump at one corner, as well as the church and village smithy beside it, and this is where the village's communal activities took place, no doubt. But the other part of the green had the village school on it and became the meeting place of the local hunt. It seems certain that these two areas formed one large green at first.

Kislingbury is an ironstone village with its small green in front of the church, bearing a tall village sign on a stepped stone base.

Badby and some other villages in this area betray by their names their Danish foundation or domination, but Denton and Ashton, in the eastern half of North-amptonshire, are Anglo-Saxon villages. Denton, with Brafield-on-the-Green next door, as it were, is an attractive little place with what I suppose could fairly be described as a village green running narrowly alongside the road through it, with a horse-trough keeping it company.

Nothing so unsightly impinges on Ashton's central neatness. The modern village owes its prettiness to a rare butterfly, the Chequered Skipper, for the Hon. Charles de Rothschild, who rebuilt the village at the turn of the century, was an entomologist of note, and he built himself a country mansion here and presented the whole village to his wife as a wedding present. The cottages of stone and thatch are gathered round a village green where each year the Conker Championship of Great Britain takes place, and no telegraph poles or wires spoil the scene, as they were mercifully laid underground when the rebuilding took place. All this good fortune was due to the fact that the Rockingham Forest area was a known habitat of the butterfly which the Hon. Charles fancied.

Titchmarsh is well known for the fine Perpendicular tower of its church, often compared with the celebrated towers of Somerset, but the village also has a green with almshouses on one side.

The triangular market-place at Higham Ferrers looks like one of those places where there was a green once, though no longer. It is close to the church and has a market cross, and a local historian only a century ago could describe the parish's one hundred cows being brought in from the common with a boy leading them and blowing a horn to warn the people they were coming.

Close to the Leicestershire border, in that part of Northamptonshire where the rock has yielded iron ore and turned the area into an industrial eyesore of quarrying and steelworks, there are many pleasant villages tucked safely away in the country lanes which show the more appealing side of the local geology – brown ironstone cottages with a warm and mellow look, often with roofs of thatch. Most of them are street villages, but Gretton has a charming triangular green ruined only by the intimidating presence of its old stocks and whipping post. The last person to sit in the stocks could have enjoyed the view of the valley below if he had been sober, but he is said to have been a drunkard, put there in 1858 to recover his sobriety.

The old county of Leicestershire was not better provided with green villages than its neighbour Northamptonshire, but its marriage with Rutland in the local government reorganization brought it a dowry of fine villages, several of them having small and attractive greens. The best known of the old county's greens is the sloping triangular one at Hallaton, supporting its conical market cross and war memorial and surrounded by thatched cottages and houses and the Bewicke Arms, all built of stone. This green, for most of the year a quiet and uneventful patch of grass, becomes on Easter Mondays the noisy and crowded centre of what seems an almost Bacchanalian orgy in certain respects, when the village holds its Hare Pie Scrambling and Bottle Kicking rituals. They invariably end up here, with someone sitting uncomfortably astride the stone cross and tipping back one of the 'bottles' – actually a frothy cask of ale which has been kicked around in a rowdy football-like game against a team from the neighbouring village of Medbourne. No question of the pagan origin of this annual ritual. The parson by custom supplies the Hare Pie which is scrambled for at Hare Pie Bank in a symbolic fertility ritual, and when the parson has in the past, and not surprisingly, objected to being involved in this primitive orgy, he has been threatened with expulsion – 'No pie, no parson' being the cryptic message from the villagers.

Nothing so vulgar disturbs the tiny triangular green at the nearby prim and proper village of Horninghold. You feel it is only with reluctance that the village sign on the green tells you where you are, but for all its stand-offishness, Horninghold is a place of rare style – a picturesque model village of mellow brown stone built by lord of the manor Thomas Hardcastle at the beginning of the century. It comes as no surprise to find that it has been a winner of the Best Kept Village competition. The only amazing thing is that it has ever had any serious rivals in the contest.

Church Langton has a featureless triangular green, as befits the 'metropolis' of the group of five Langton villages; and Buckminster, up in the north-east corner near the Lincolnshire border, has a rectangular green of fair size shaded by venerable trees, with a row of terraced cottages along one side. Knipton and Muston, in the Vale of Belvoir, may not be green villages for much longer, when coal dust starts to spread its deathly grey pall over this beautiful area.

Great Bowden and Beeby also retain their greens in the eastern half of the old county, but one would expect the western half, which is mainly arable land, to have more greens than the rolling pastures of the east. This expectation is not fulfilled, however. Industry has taken over the villages of west Leicestershire, except in the Charnwood Forest area, and greens do not long survive the urban needs of factory workers. I can remember a small green at the centre of Barwell, where the buses stopped on their way to Leicester, but it has gone now, and the greens of the western half of the county are represented only by the patches of grass at such as Belton and Mountsorrel, both noted for their annual fairs. The grassy area on either side of the Rothley Brook which flows through Anstey may or may not properly qualify as a village green, but it is interesting for the medieval stone pack-horse bridge on it, now used only by pedestrians as it has been replaced by a modern road bridge nearby, but it was probably built by the Grey family of Bradgate Park to facilitate their journeys into Leicester.

When we too travel east and cross over into what used to be the county of Rutland, things look up a bit in quality, if not in quantity. Lyddington, just across the border from Hallaton and Horninghold, has a good-sized green with the broken column of a village cross on its pedestal, and some nice ironstone houses round it, though the bus shelter and children's swings at one side do nothing to help its picturesque qualities.

Left: Collingham, Nottinghamshire. An attractive view from the village green in a county hardly noted for its rural scenes.

Below: Heydon, Norfolk. One of the most attractive of the county's green villages, with an unusually elaborate well-head housing of brick.

Left: Linton, North Yorkshire. A fine spot summer relaxation in village noted for some buildings near its well-kept green.

Below: Nun Monkton, North Yorkshire. Graz rights are still maintai on this roughly triang green with a pond wh livestock are watered.

Children would have danced on the well-known turf maze at Wing on Easter Mondays at one time. No one has ever suggested, to my knowledge, that this forty-foot circle was ever a village green, but we perhaps ought to bear the possibility in mind. An absurd belief has grown up about the few surviving mazes in England that they are of Christian origin, used as a form of penance for errant monks. But in *A Midsummer Night's Dream* Shakespeare says that,

> The nine-men's morris is fill'd up with
> mud;
> And the quaint mazes in the wanton
> green,
> For lack of tread, are undistinguishable.

This implies that many such turf mazes have been lost, and we actually know of some of them – there was once one at Priestly Hill near Lyddington, which was ploughed up. Shakespeare does not appear to have believed in any link with Christianity, and nor do I. These mazes were of more ancient and pagan origin and partly explain why Shakespeare's green is 'wanton', as well as indicating that the village green is where they were usually to be found. So perhaps the fenced-in maze at the roadside in Wing is the carefully preserved remnant of a once larger green. At any rate, a festive ritual of some sort, related to maypole dancing, was practised on such mazes all over Britain and got them known as 'Troy Town' by association with Greece through the Cretan Labyrinth, where Theseus rescued the Athenian maidens from the dread Minotaur.

Braunston's green is shaded by fine trees, while Exton's has a circle of sycamores and some thatched cottages round it as well as the Fox and Hounds, an apt name in these parts, where any village green that is large enough is likely to see a gathering of red-coated riders during the winter months, the Cottesmore Hunt holding authority in this territory.

The small green at Market Overton has the village stocks and whipping post on it, and one who probably saw several miserable felons with blood running down their backs from the lashes meted out here was the young Isaac Newton, whose mother was born in the village and whose grandmother looked after the budding mathematician before he went to Cambridge.

Cambridgeshire, like Leicestershire, has added a few greens to its sparse collection through the Local Government Act. We have already noticed the absence of greens in the fenlands, and the greens of old Cambridgeshire were limited to a few in the vicinity of Cambridge itself, with one or two surprising exceptions. Wicken, out in the fens and now well known to naturalists as an area which land-reclamation left relatively untouched, has two greens, although the village is stretched out along a main road. One is rectangular, and there is a smaller, triangular one with a duck-pond. The National Trust land Wicken stands by is now higher than the surrounding area because it has not been drained and thus shrunken, and a windmill which elsewhere would have pumped water *out* is here used to pump water *in* to preserve the fen's medieval character. Wicken is one of the exceptions which prove the rule about greens in the fens, however, and we must go some way south to the larger villages of Barrington and Babraham, south of Cambridge, for the classic greens of the old county, although the green at Reach, near Wicken, should not go unnoticed, as it was created specially at some relatively late stage in the settlement's development by levelling out part of the ancient earthwork called Devil's Dyke. This undertaking was presumably a response to medieval population pressure.

Barrington's green is actually a common – a long and shapeless twenty-two-acre affair which would have been even bigger if some settlement and enclosure had not occurred in the seventeenth century. It has the village church at one end and the windmill near the opposite side, with a path through the middle called the 'Church Path' and cottages along both sides, but it is ruined by telegraph poles and cables crossing it, to say nothing of a winding road that meets up with others to form a junction near the church. Barrington's green has been cited as one of the enclosed type that, in the north, have been taken as 'defensive' village centres, but we can scarcely postulate border troubles as the source of this green's shape

Left: Moreton Pinkney, Northamptonshire. Th[e] winding road through [the] village wove its way between squatters' cottages on the origina[l] green, leaving little mo[re] than wide grass verges[.]

Right: Badby, Northamptonshire. Go[ese] help to keep the grass down on this large irregular green crisscrossed by roads a[nd] pathways.

and arrangement. Babraham (corrupted from the original Badburgham) has chestnut trees shading its green.

These are villages of ancient foundation (there was a Saxon burial ground near Barrington's green, and between them lies Great Shelford which, though less attractive than either, is interesting for having once had two triangular greens, High Green and Ashen Green, which have been enclosed and built upon.

Another partly lost green was at Comberton, and for those readers who are sceptical of my interpretation of Shakespeare's reference to mazes, here is evidence, for Comberton's green had a maze on it until relatively recently, larger than Wing's. But by 1930 it had been enclosed as part of the village school's playground and was, naturally enough, worn away after a few years.

Histon, to the north of Cambridge, is now virtually a city suburb, but it retains a substantial area of green on either bank of the river flowing through it, with some thatched cottages alongside.

One of the villages which Cambridgeshire has acquired, or, to be more accurate, re-acquired in this particular case, is Thorney. It *was* in Cambridgeshire, then went to Huntingdonshire and the Soke of Peterborough and is now in Cambridgeshire again. The original ancient settlement was an 'island' in the middle of the marshes, an ideal place for the establishment of a monastery, which was destroyed by the heathen Danes, then re-established and much lauded in medieval times. After the

Anstey, Leicestershire. The medieval packhorse bridge across the Rothley Brook gives only pedestrian access, these days, to the green banks on either side

Dissolution the abbey properties passed to the Earls of Bedford. It was the fourth Earl who was most active and ambitious in engaging the Dutch engineer Vermuyden to reclaim so much of this land from the sea. Thorney now stands in what has ever since been known as the Bedford Level, about a crossroads in this flat and treeless geometrical landscape. But Thorney itself has trees on account of its being a model village rebuilt by the then Duke of Bedford, and its small green is surrounded by elegant houses, including the vicarage, built of stone from the abbey. The green here is square, and the reason is that it was formerly the cloister of the abbey, the church nave of which stands nearby, still in use as the parish church, having been restored by the Earl of Bedford for the labourers who came to work in recovering the submerged land here.

Ramsey – likewise in Huntingdonshire until recently – also had its monastery, this one a larger and more powerful house than Thorney's. But it was even less fortunate after the Dissolution, being entirely dismantled by the Cromwells except for a fragment of the great gatehouse, which still stands beside Abbey Green. If this turf was never a true village green when Ramsey was just a village, it has much of the character of one now that Ramsey is a market town.

Yaxley, Farcet and Orton Waterville are among other small greens which have passed from Peterborough to Cambridgeshire, while Helpston has been tossed about from county to county like a ball, having enjoyed the protection of Northampton-shire as well as Huntingdonshire before coming to Cambridgeshire. It was in Nor-thamptonshire when John Clare was born here in 1793, the son of a farm labourer, and the young peasant was familiar with the ancient stone cross on the green and the stone cottages all round. He was born in one of them himself, down the road next to the Bluebell Inn. He knew the churchyard nearby, too, and was laid to rest in it in 1864 when his tormented life was over. He was a true poet of nature, poor in material things but rich in his appreciation of the simple life around him. As a boy he became so absorbed in the nature of the village's surroundings that he would come home late and find his parents distraught and half the villagers out searching for him. It was a dissociation from normal human contact that was prophetic of the mental illness that was to plague him for nearly half his life:

> With other boys he little cared to mix;
> Joy left him lonely in his hawthorn bowers . . .

He was an acute observer, never a joiner in the communal activities of the village:

> . . . dear to him the rural sports of May,
> When each cot. threshold mounts its hailing
> bough,
> And ruddy milkmaids weave their garlands gay,
> Upon the green to crown the earliest cow,
> When mirth and pleasure wear a joyful brow,
> And join the tumult with unbounded glee
> The humble tenants of the pale and plough:
> He lov'd 'old sports', by them reviv'd, to see,
> But never car'd to join in their rude revelry.

Now where the milkmaids wove their garlands a monument stands on the green to the village poet, close to the old cross he knew so well.

Suffolk and Norfolk are better off for greens than the fens and the Midlands and in some respects continue that quantity and variety we have followed through eastern England from Kent and Essex. One of the best-known greens in England is just over the Suffolk border from Essex at Cavendish, in the valley of the River Stour. The spacious, sloping green with neatly thatched and colour-washed cottages at the top, with church tower rising behind them, is among the most photographed greens in the whole country, and many people probably associate the place mentally with laburnum in full bloom beside the cottage walls.

We should take note of a theory about the greens of East Anglia here: that they were frequently established on damp ground to provide pasture and that, as the

demand for more fertile soil increased, village centres shifted to these relatively unproductive spots to release more valuable land for cultivation.

A little way to the east of Cavendish is Long Melford, a street village stretched out along a junction of main roads, but it is a place of style distinguished for its many fine buildings, one of which, the Elizabethan Melford Hall, stands with its back turned to the green behind a high wall with an elaborate gateway in it. The green is also long, and triangular in shape, with the Victorian village school at the bottom end and the splendid 'wool church' at the top, and houses of both modest and ambitious dimensions in between. There is a pit in it from which itinerant brick-makers dug clay for making the bricks that went into Melford Hall, and among other buildings round it are the Elizabethan almshouses of brick, known as Trinity Hospital, built by Sir William Cordell for twelve poor men and two women, who must have gained some comfort in their last days from the lovely scene they looked out on. Perhaps the most curious of all the buildings on this green, however, is the brick conduit, near the gates to the hall, which is believed to have been the source of the manor house's original water supply.

This green was a traditional meeting-place of gypsies and the site of a horse fair, and it was well known to George Borrow, who – according to his own account in *Lavengro* – met his tall mistress Isopel Berners in the company of gypsies in this vicinity and learned that she was born in the 'great house of Long Melford'.

Hawkedon is not far away, with its church curiously imprisoned, as it seems, in the middle of the green, with the houses all round keeping guard over it. At Monks Eleigh, over to the east, the parish pump occupies the honoured position on a much smaller green lined by houses with the church at the top, while Polstead's green is at the top of a hill, with Corder's Farm among the cottages clustered round it. Here lived William Corder, the murderer of Maria Marten in the notorious 'Red Barn' case of 1828, and how often the villagers must have seen murderer and victim walking across this green before both their lives were ended so abruptly.

Farther north, Woolpit has a very small, triangular green at its centre with a pump which is housed beneath a conical tiled roof supported on wooden posts adorned with little bronze statues. This was put up in 1897 to commemorate Queen Victoria's Diamond Jubilee. The Swan Inn overlooks the green, built in 1759 with a later upper storey and once a busy staging post for coaches travelling between Stowmarket and Bury St Edmunds, but now rather quieter as the main road bypasses the village centre.

Euston, near the Norfolk border, sounds like a busy place but is in fact a sleepy village built largely of flint and thatch to house the estate workers of the Duke of Grafton's Euston Hall, and it has much green about it without anything in the nature of an original nucleus, for the old settlements were destroyed here in the course of enclosing the park.

Burgate is one of the Suffolk villages which have more than one green. There are no fewer than five here, and even the smallest, called Little Green, reasonably enough, is larger than many of the tiny greens we have encountered elsewhere.

The Swan at Hoxne (pronounced Hoxen) is older than Woolpit's but also stands near a triangular green in the fork of the roads. Maybe the green was here – though the inn was not – when the East Anglian martyr King Edmund was killed with arrows by the Danes, not far from here in AD 870.

Cottages surround the green at Wingfield, with the fortified manor house of the Poles, Wingfield Castle, nearby among the trees and surrounded by a moat; while at Earl Soham, a farmhouse near the green has the remains of some wall paintings of classical subjects done in the eighteenth century. The village sign on the green here was erected in 1953 to mark the coronation of Queen Elizabeth II.

Orford, on the coast to the south-east, was an important port once but declined to village status as the sea receded from it. Quay Street has a long green with the Jolly Sailor at the end of it, but the white-painted village pump is on a tiny patch of green in Pump Street.

ldington, Leicester-
re. The remains of the
dieval market cross
nd on the highest point
his Rutland green.

Histon, Cambridgeshire. A spacious green area traversed by a tributary of the River Ouse, with cottages well spread out.

A little way inland to the north, the very large green at Westleton is of more traditional appearance. It is subject to common rights but is used for communal activities, including an annual fair, and has a village duckpond, thatched church, windmill and Crown Inn nearby.

Greens in coastal resorts may be treated with caution and Southwold is a case in point. This small town figures as 'Swoul' in the local verse Defoe found current here:

> Swoul and Dunwich, and Walderswick,
> All go in at one lousie creek

Fulbeck, Lincolnshire. The restored church cross in a village where a sloping green with pump is overlooked by the gargoyles on the village church and – even more ugly – many wires and cables.

th, Nottinghamshire. e village is a busy place pite being bypassed by A1, but it still has its asant central green.

The creek is the mouth of the River Blyth, and its gradual closing up by the natural formation of a barrier of sand brought a decline in the sea trade which was the *raison d'être* of the towns and villages here. Then in 1659 there was a disastrous fire at Southwold, which consumed the public buildings and more than two hundred houses, and it was after this that the rebuilding was done on a plan which included seven open spaces called South Green, North Green, East Green, St Edmund's Green and St James's Green, Barnaby Green and Bartholomew Green. So, although guide-books say that Southwold keeps much of its 'olde worlde' charm about it, which indeed it does, with narrow streets and picturesque buildings, its old pump is ironically in the triangular market-place, which *may* have been the original green, and the present greens are of modern conception. The several greens at Ilketshall St Andrew are genuine old greens but are all classified as commons, though one of them, Holdens Green, is hardly larger than the Little Green at Burgate.

The last of the notable Suffolk greens is at Somerleyton, in the north-east corner of the county, and it is also a modern creation, with a Victorian pump of iron on a square green which is fenced in. The unlikely benefactor of this remote East Anglian village was a railway magnate, Sir Samuel Morton Peto, who also built Nelson's Column. Pevsner calls his model village 'weird', but others regard it as picturesque, even 'perfect'. The green, at any rate, is extensive, with cottages and village school grouped round it.

Although there is a distinct lack of greens in east Norfolk, especially around the

Broads, we can cross the border to find one green easily enough at Toft Monks, where the three-acre green which is, strictly speaking, a common, is nevertheless known as Maypole Green – an uncompromising enough name implying long use as a communal space.

Old and New Buckenham, farther west, both have their greens, but what a contrast in styles we find in these neighbouring villages! Old Buckenham's Church Green is a huge affair of twenty acres, complete with ponds, though there is a smaller green here as well, the village being a scattered place made up of several hamlets, each with its own centre. New Buckenham was new only in medieval times, when the lord of the manor, William d'Albini, abandoned his castle and 'Old' Buckenham and built a new one two miles away. In contrast to the haphazard growth of the old village, the 'new' one is neatly planned with a central green and an old market hall on it with a cobbled floor. One of the timber columns supporting the upper storey of this building doubled as a whipping post. The clock on the church tower peeps across the green over the roofs of the houses on one side.

Banham has a fine green which used to be graced by tall elms but still has its timber-framed guildhall with overhanging upper storey, and other attractive buildings round it, as well as the village church. East Bradenham's green has a cricket pitch on it. West Acre, north of Swaffham, has a church clock near the rough green at the village centre, with the words 'Watch and pray' taking the place of the usual numerals on its face. Several thatched houses round the green lend a peaceful atmosphere to this place where a former priory had its entrance from the green.

There was also a priory at Great Massingham in this county which was always well endowed with religious houses, and the ponds on the village green here are probably the monastery's old fish ponds. The green is split up by roadways and its attractiveness spoilt by tasteless building. Heydon has an attractive green with a brick pump-house on it and the flint church close by, with a gabled house beside it which is said to have been the former bakehouse of the manor house.

Near the coast to the north, Burnham Market, Burnham Overy and Burnham Thorpe sport greens with stylish houses round them, Thorpe's being obviously known to Nelson, who was born there, although it is not at the centre of the village; and Wells-next-the-Sea has a rectangular green with trees round it. Narrow alleys lead from it to the village church of St Nicholas. This green is called 'The Buttlands', which indicates one of its early uses clearly enough, but the one at Cley-next-the-Sea, similarly pushed back from the water's edge by land reclamation, is ominously called 'Newgate Green'. Newgate, however, is in this case merely the name of the district south of the town centre, where Cley's fine church stands, and indicates the entrance from the medieval village to the modern nucleus.

Among other Norfolk villages nicely gathered round their greens are Wilton, Methwold, East Tuddenham and Horsham St Faith. Norfolk and Suffolk are the last of the counties where we can expect to find the quaint descriptive or frankly baffling names given to green villages in the south-eastern quarter of England, and in Suffolk we have Magpie Green, Silverlace Green and Brussels Green, among others, while Norfolk offers Dumpling Green, Gorse Green and Brewers Green.

The paucity of village greens in the Cambridgeshire fens continues through Lincolnshire, and such greens as that county possesses tend to be on the western side along and around the limestone belt that runs northward through Stamford and Lincoln. Castle Bytham is near the Leicestershire border, an attractive village of stone walls and red pantile roofs, but its green is tiny and insignificant, and this is the pattern we shall find throughout a county which once had many more greens but has lost them through enclosure, road-widening operations and so on. Newton is one example of a village which has lost its green to all intents and purposes. Inn, cottages and a farmhouse stand in a central area with a stream running through it on what was clearly once an open green of oval shape, with the church, school and village cross beside it.

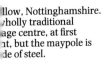

llow, Nottinghamshire. wholly traditional age centre, at first nt, but the maypole is de of steel.

Folkingham still has some green of sorts at its centre, but it is formalized into a spacious square, dominated by the Greyhound, an elegant Georgian coaching inn of brick at the top end, for the place was on the Peterborough–Lincoln road and developed into a market town, with its own House of Correction where a Norman castle had once stood.

Much the same sort of thing has happened at Heckington, famous for its windmill with eight sails. The original green had a market cross on it which has been re-erected in the churchyard in the process of turning the green area into a car-park.

Kelby is among the large number of villages founded by the Danes in these parts, but ironically this is more like a traditional Anglo-Saxon village with a green and duckpond at its centre. But it is at Fulbeck that Lincolnshire suddenly restores our fading interest, for this is a very attractive village of stone with a street running gently uphill from the valley of the River Witham to a hilltop green with the church overlooking the village pump and cottages of warm stone and orange pantiles. The church tower has eight pinnacles and much fine medieval carving in limestone, including gargoyles that have gazed down for seven hundred years on the peaceful green below, lying quietly off the main road.

Scopwick is really a street village which has a long, narrow stretch of green with a stream running through it, but on the whole our search for green villages will not be much more productive in this large county, and we shall do well to move on elsewhere, for there are hardly more than twenty acres of green in all the villages of this huge area of England.

Nottinghamshire is, if anything, even less rewarding in our present context. Clifton's green is notable for its large dovecote of brick and the almshouses of the early eighteenth century which face it. Car Colston has a pleasant and sizeable green, and South Collingham presents an unmistakable Midlands scene with its houses of red brick, while Blyth, up in the north of the county, seems lucky still to have its triangular green when it has become a junction of so many roads.

A main road passes through Wellow, near Ollerton, but this village remains attractive and has a maypole on the green, which has some pleasant individual houses round it and the church tower rising behind them. It is surprising to find one of England's few remaining permanent maypoles in this industrial county, but on close examination it turns out to be made of steel. An important part of the old May Day tradition was the cutting and carrying of the birch sapling from the wood (in Wellow's case, Sherwood Forest), but even pagan ceremonies are now subject to industrial interference. Why not, I ask myself, a plastic replica of the village stocks?

—VII—

The North East

HUMBERSIDE, YORKSHIRE, CLEVELAND, DURHAM, TYNE & WEAR, NORTHUMBERLAND

The Midlands have shown us a gap in the consistency of green villages. Compared with the south-east, there are fewer of them, and they are of more scrappy and shapeless appearance. But as we reach the north of England, village greens are re-established with a vengeance, becoming more regular in terms of both number of them and their shape. This does not happen in the industrial areas of Humberside and South Yorkshire, however. South of the Humber, the scarcity of greens in old Lincolnshire continues, and we have to cross the new bridge and turn left to Welton to find the first green worthy of note. An attractive pond is near the green and the churchyard, and the green supports a Victorian stone pump. Perhaps it was on or near the green that John Palmer shot his landlord's cockerel out of malice in 1738? He got himself arrested and turned out to be none other than Dick Turpin. He had lived in Welton for two years and earned himself some local respect, but this stupid act set him on the road to the gallows at York.

North Newbald has two greens – one small and shapeless and the other larger and square, with trees on one side and houses on the other three; but it is Bishop Burton, five miles to the east, that easily claims all the honours among Humberside village greens. It is split up by roadways and a fenced-in pond of crescent shape, with attractive cottages and stone walls scattered haphazardly about it, half hidden by magnificent chestnut trees. There is an old pump and a war memorial, and the church stands above them all on a hill. The only noise at this otherwise peaceful village centre might be the cackle of geese around the pond, but a human voice was heard loud and clear on this green in the eighteenth century, when John Wesley preached to such good effect that the villagers established an annual service on the green to commemorate the occasion, and had a bust of Wesley carved from the tree under which he preached to them.

137

A little way north is Lund, where a triangular green supports a beheaded market cross and the depression of the old village cock-fighting pit, while over to the west near the new Yorkshire border Bishop Wilton and Stamford Bridge have their respective greens, the latter uncompromisingly northern, with a brick pub and a chip shop among its neighbours, and the former a little unusual in having a stream running through its length, bisecting both green and village, with a road and houses flanking the rough sloping banks.

We have seen that there are few parts of the eastern side of England that cannot show one or two respectable old village greens here and there, and even South Yorkshire is not entirely devoid of them, notwithstanding the smoke and coal dust that pervade the air almost everywhere within reach of Sheffield, Barnsley, Rotherham and Doncaster. Shafton, for instance, has a green of eight acres, subject to common rights, though even a hundred years ago the only livestock you might expect to come across in this region would be resting pit ponies.

We ought not to expect West Yorkshire to provide much in the way of green villages either, but Havercroft has one even bigger than Shafton's, although it, too, is arguably a common. Barwick-in-Elmet, with its permanent maypole in the market-place, is just one of the villages which have lost their former greens in this industrial landscape; but Seacroft, now within the eastern boundary of Leeds, still has its 5½-acre green with the Cricketers Arms at the old village centre, where the annual fair is held. With a suburban population of sixty thousand, and urban litter on the ground and tower blocks in the sky, the green can hardly be described as still semi-rural, but at least it is still there, and West Yorkshire has one or two more surprises in store for us.

Heath, near Wakefield, is a village of fine merchants' houses built round the large green by the *nouveaux riches* of the Industrial Revolution; while at Ackworth, subject to mining subsidence, the village church stands beside the green along with some remarkably good houses and an eighteenth-century almshouse, and a partly medieval village cross is on the green itself. Thorp Arch also has a pleasant green within a stone's throw of Wetherby.

It is when we pass into North Yorkshire, however, that the real delights of Yorkshire's village greens await us, with their enormous variety of shape, size and scene. Askham Richard has an irregular green largely taken up by a sizeable duckpond which is usually occupied by a variety of wildfowl, and the Rose and Crown stands nearby to refresh the human visitors.

A tall maypole stands on the long, broad green at Nun Monkton, where an avenue leads from the green with its surrounding brick cottages to the church, which is the only remaining part (the original nave) of a nunnery founded here in the twelfth

st Witton, North
orkshire. A characteristic
een of these parts, with
uses huddling round it
a close-knit village
cleus.

sington, Derbyshire.
lish houses of pale
estone enhance the
en centre of this very
ractive model village.

Bempton, Humberside.
The village is near the
coast not far from
Bridlington, and its green
attracts various sea-birds.

century – hence the village name. When the road reaches the river (the Nidd joins the Ouse here), it ends abruptly, and you have to turn round and go back the way you came, so the village is a peaceful place except when the duck population is giving full voice to its good fortune in having so much water to paddle in and plenty of gardens in which to lay eggs. The ducks do not have exclusive rights to this pond, however. The green, which is a long triangle squeezed in the middle like a bonny Yorkshire lass, is evidently subject to common rights which are still exercised, and cattle still drink from the pond as they have probably done for a thousand years.

No such rustic continuity is to be seen at Hillam, alas, to the south of Tadcaster. This village's fate is typical of the industrial north and the Midlands. A triangle of grass is still there at its centre, but it has been reduced to such a ludicrous size by road improvements that one wonders who would want to sit under the chestnut tree on what looks more like a traffic island than a village green, with white lines all round it. Perhaps only the unemployed with nothing better to do. As Hillam is near the Selby coalfield, the writing is on the wall for this hopelessly non-communal bit of grass and others like it.

I must mention the small green at Appleton Roebuck, if only to draw attention to the unusually lyrical name of this village in the gritty north of England; and New Earswick, just outside York, is a model village built mainly, though not exclusively, for the workers at Rowntree's in 1902, and it has a large modern green at the centre. Sheriff Hutton, on the other hand, a few miles north, has its main street climbing towards the North York Moors past the ancient green, with the Norman castle dominating the scene from above.

Aldborough stands on the site of a Roman camp called Iseurium Brigantium. Iseur was the Celtic headquarters of the Brigantes, that tribe which was a constant thorn in the side of the Roman army of occupation, but though there are Roman remains to be seen here, the only relic of the pagan Celts seems to be the symbolic maypole on the small sloping village green, which is called 'The Square' and is surrounded by brick houses, with some steps that lead to the remains of the former court-house where election results were read out in the days when this 'rotten borough' had two Members of Parliament. The green is a peaceful place today, but although it was formed well after the Roman departure, it was long a scene of preparation for warfare, as the villagers made longbows from the yew trees in the churchyard and practised their archery here.

Howsham is the tiny toffee-coloured village where George Hudson, 'the Railway King', was born, and it has a diminutive green in keeping with its own modest size, with the old village pump close beside its cottages.

Langton is an attractive stone-built village with a wide green looking towards the Wolds and having a faintly aristocratic air with the manor house gates on it, and indeed, the place is an estate village built by the Norcliffe family, lords of the manor in the nineteenth century; while Hovingham, also built of creamy-grey limestone, has a shapeless green winding between the houses of an elegant village much influenced by the presence of the Worsley family's great house there. The main area of green is a long stretch fenced in white alongside the road facing the Worsley Arms Hotel, a Georgian coaching inn. A triangular green with the war memorial is separated from it by the village school, and a little stream trickles along beside it.

The greens at Crayke and Husthwaite are slightly untypical of these parts in having houses of brick and even half-timbering around them, although they are quite unlike each other, Husthwaite's being a pocket-handkerchief-size triangle, railed in, with a tree, seat and signpost upon it, and Crayke's larger, sloping and more open, with the village church looking down on it from a hilltop. The controversial Dean of St Paul's, William Inge, was born in this village and knew the green well enough, for he often watched cricket being played on it.

At Hutton-le-Hole and Lastingham, up on the moors proper, we find a startling contrast. These delightful villages were both here at the time of the Domesday survey, but Hutton-le-Hole was developed by Quaker ironmasters in the seventeenth and eighteenth centuries and is now one of Yorkshire's most beautiful villages. The vast green on which it is set is really a common, with the cottages of grey stone and red pantile roofs scattered about it in haphazard fashion. Roads and pathways between them are separated from the greens by little white fences, and white wooden bridges cross the stream, with sheep grazing freely anywhere they care to wander. Lastingham is much tighter and older-looking, its tiny triangular greens sprinkled about like a miniature Hutton-le-Hole.

Rosedale, sometimes called Rosedale Abbey on account of the Cistercian priory that once stood here, became an industrial village involved in iron mining later, but now clusters round its green in rural isolation in the valley of the River Seven, with the village church and school close by. Up on the moors to the north-east, meanwhile, Goathland also occupies a lonely position if you ignore the Fylingdales 'radomes' and the staff who operate the 'early warning' system there. Goathland is an attractive and well spread-out village with its pantiled cottages scattered over a large, irregular green.

Now we come to Lealholm and Danby, where sheep graze up to the cottage doors as in most of the moorland villages, and little bridges cross the streams tumbling down from the higher ground carpeted with heather.

It is worth reminding ourselves at this point of the theory of defensive origin of

Bishop Burton, Humberside. One of the most attractive of northern greens, it has a thriving population of ducks on its pond.

Stamford Bridge, Humberside. The railed-in green has the Bide A Wee inn as its rather arch neighbour.

village greens, for soon we shall be in the thick of the areas which lend most force to that proposition, but it is quite clear that no such idea dictated the layout of villages up on the moorland here. Great Ayton and Hutton Rudby continue the picture of northern openness, with two greens, High and Low, at the former village and one large one at the latter. The Royal Oak stands by High Green at Great Ayton, along with the village pump and horse-trough, and the young James Cook sat on this green and maybe dreamed of faraway places, his imagination following the water of the River Leven on its course towards the sea and the great oceans beyond. The Quaker school, which also faces the green, was not here then, having been built in 1842, but the older village school where Cook got his primary education is still here, unlike the cottage he lived in, which was dismantled and shipped to Australia. The Leven flows through Rudby-in-Cleveland on its way to join the Tees, and separates it from Hutton Rudby on the opposite bank, where a long, shapeless green accompanies the stream through the village.

Osmotherley's triangular green is another of those from which John Wesley preached, by the village cross where a stone table used for market wares served as his pulpit. He had no doubt heard the Lyke Wake Dirge, with which the souls of the dead were launched on their supposed journey across the moors, and whatever he may have thought of it, the Dirge has given rise to the Lyke Wake Walk, which starts from this green and involves a trek of forty miles to Ravenscar.

In the opposite direction are the Pennine dales, with many interesting village greens worthy of attention, such as those at Linton and Burnsall in Wharfedale, both past winners of competitions for best village awards. Linton is indeed a stylish place, with modest houses round a shapeless green presided over by two grander buildings which seem to me like a society host and hostess lording it over their guests, with the Fountain Inn serving the drinks. One of these buildings is the manor house, Linton Hall, and the other Fountaine's Hospital, built by the lord of the manor, Richard Fountaine, for six poor women, and designed by Sir John Vanbrugh, no less, for Fountaine was his friend and timber-merchant. Nearby is an old packhorse bridge over the beck.

Burnsall's green has a maypole on it and is the starting point for the August Bank Holiday race up Burnsall Fell and back, a run not to be undertaken lightly. The river runs alongside the green here, and further upstream is Conistone, where cottages are gathered round a small green.

horp Arch, West
orkshire. This attractive
een village is
rprisingly well preserved
nong the industrial
wns of the former West
ding.

Arncliffe is a little more isolated in Littondale and, although attractive, has a little more northern ruggedness, with stone cottages roofed with stone slabs round its long green. An old guidebook dismisses the village as having 'hardly anything of interest', but that is only if your preoccupation is with grand or ecclesiastical architecture. Arncliffe's green usually has livestock of one sort or another keeping its grass short, as it did, no doubt, in the very earliest days of the settlement. The village had its own cotton-mill once, and the green's Falcon Inn was the original hostelry in Yorkshire TV's soap opera *Emmerdale Farm*.

At Bainbridge, to the north, the large green is the site of an ancient and laudable custom in a village that shows its sturdy independence in more than one way. The place has no church, to begin with. It became a centre for Quakers but was not so unorthodox as not to have its village stocks, which are made of stone. But while other places were building their steeple-houses, Bainbridge kept up a more practical custom by sounding a hunting horn on the green at nine o'clock on winter evenings to guide travellers lost on the hostile fells, though those who support the defensive origin of village greens reckon it was originally a medieval signal to shepherds to bring their flocks into the village centre for the night. But surely shepherds would have known when to do that without being told.

In these parts, as everywhere else in England at one time, the village blacksmith was the community's most important craftsman, and it went almost without saying that the forge was always at the centre of the village beside the green, if not invariably beneath a spreading chestnut tree. The smith was held in such high esteem by ancient peoples that he was raised to the pantheon of their gods – Hephaestos to the Greeks; Vulcan to the Romans; Volund or Wayland to the Scandinavians. He was always represented as being lame, and though this was explained in the myths as due to assorted misadventures, it was perhaps because constant standing at the anvil made his legs weak compared with his strong arms and shoulders, though you would hardly think so from the images of village blacksmiths in village cricket fiction, 'breasting the slope superbly', as A. G. Macdonell has it, for instance, 'like a mettlesome combination of Vulcan and Venus Anadyomene'.

The farrier's eminence arose not merely because he was an expert on the all-important horse (and, before that, the ox) but also because he made the tools for all the other village craftsmen and workers – the carpenter, mason, thatcher, wheelwright, farmer and so on. He also made the spurs which the village men fixed to the heels of their fighting cocks during a main in a bloody dip at the corner

Askham Richard, North Yorkshire. The duckpond occupies a considerable area of the green in this quiet village near York.

of the green. Not only did he shoe the horses (making his own tools and nails as well as the shoes) but he was often the local horse-doctor as well, and as travellers through the village were apt to spend time at the smithy waiting while their horses were shod, the anvil became for the men what the pump or the well was for the women: a rendezvous for gossip and exchanging news and opinions. The people gathered at the smithy might include a farmer having his plough repaired, a mason calling for a new chisel he had ordered, a carpenter wanting a saw, a stranger passing through whose horse had cast a shoe on the road, and always a few of the old men and young boys of the village for whom the furnace, the clanking of hammer on anvil, the shock of steam as red-hot iron was quenched in cold water, the flying sparks and the lively talk, were irresistible magnets, as large holes in the ground are to unoccupied men today. On rare occasions, they might be joined by the parson, who wished the blacksmith to put a new hinge on the church door, or one of the village women wanting a repair to her cooking range.

Nowadays, though the blacksmith still exists and is as skilful as he ever was, he has been relegated from his former eminence by the Industrial Revolution and

rnsall, North Yorkshire.
e Pennine fells rise
ove this delightful
harfedale village with its
tensive riverside green
here local games are
ld in August.

only rarely occupies his time-honoured position at the village centre, if he works in the village at all. He may spend his time shoeing children's ponies and making wrought-iron gates and decorative lamps, and the Old Forge may now be a restaurant or an antique shop, while the smith himself has to provide a mobile service to farmers and others over a wide area. But the smith is often remembered on the village green by the sign of the inn which was once his neighbour, for 'The Horseshoes' and 'The Blacksmith's Arms' are still common pub names everywhere.

West Burton has one of the largest greens in Yorkshire, a huge and more or less oblong area with rugged cottages of grey stone around it and an early Victorian stone obelisk on it. Redmire, in Wensleydale, has a green with a lamp superimposed on a Victorian pillar on top of the medieval stepped base of a lost village cross. The King's Arms stands by the green here, which also has some nice trees on it. There are some attractive stone-built cottages around, and the green itself is large and spacious, and traversed by roads and paths. Like so many of the northern moorland

greens, it is subject to common rights and usually has the odd pony or goat tethered to it.

We have already noticed the long green at East Witton as one of those which lends some dubious support to the idea that greens were meant for defensive purposes. The old pump on it is now surmounted by a boulder that has a tap set into it, and the houses round it are separated from one another only by the paths to their backs, but I remain sceptical of the theory that medieval villagers 'closed' the village centre for protection from predators – either animal or human – and we shall need to consider the idea further as we continue northwards.

ensworth, North
kshire. An irregular
sizeable green in this
age near the county's
thern extremity.

It will not be at Ravensworth or at Aldbrough that this consideration forces itself on our attention, however. Ravensworth's spacious green of six acres has no definite shape to it and is only loosely enclosed by houses in a variety of sizes and materials. It slopes down to the scant remains of a Norman castle and overlooks the valley beyond, with the church of Kirby Hill on the opposite side. Aldbrough, meanwhile (not to be confused with the aforementioned Aldborough), is divided into two by a trickling tributary of the Tees, with a five-arch bridge linking the north green with the south green. Aldbrough St Paul is one side, Aldbrough St John the other, and the spaciousness of their greens with stone houses around defies any defensive interpretation of this village, though pagan reverence for the local water supply once offended the ecclesiastical court, when nine men were brought before it for holding a well-dressing ceremony during prayer-time, coming near the church with 'such a noyse of pyping, blowynge of an horne, ringynge or strykinge of basons and showtinge of people that the minister was constreyned to leave off readinge of prayer'.

Excuses for noisy processions are still characteristic of these parts, as we cross the border into Durham, where a whole crop of interesting greens awaits us in an area that most people, particularly in the south, associate only with coal mining and other heavy industry.

Gainford and Piercebridge lie close together on the north side of the Tees, which still forms the boundary between North Yorkshire and Durham upstream as far as Gainford. Here we are introduced to the typical Durham village with a vengeance. If you drive through it on the main road, you may be forgiven for thinking that we have gone completely off course in looking for the green villages of England. You need to turn off this road to find a roughly rectangular long village green which at once reinforces the view of anyone half inclined to accept the defensive theory. The three-acre green is almost completely closed in by the houses facing it, and it is on two levels – High and Low Greens – with trees on it and the parish church at one corner.

Piercebridge's green also has trees on it and is more accurately rectangular, with stone and colour-washed houses of assorted sizes keeping the church company around it. This was a Roman site, at an important crossing of the river, and the village occupies the ground on which a large Roman fort was built in the late third or early fourth century. The fact that the green occupies the site of the fort is sufficient proof that we cannot ascribe this green, at any rate, to foundation by the Romans, and the settlement may have been founded by British villagers soon after the Roman departure from Britain but would have been expanded and laid out later on Anglo-Saxon lines. At any rate, this is now one of the classic Durham greens in its size, shape and situation, as well as one of the most attractive greens in the far north of England, and visitors to Gainford and Piercebridge who think of the northern villages as hard streets of smoke-blackened terraced workers' houses are in for a most pleasant surprise here.

Downstream, Hurworth-on-Tees has a very long green beside the main road, with the manor house and many other solid and dignified houses beside it, some of them

ft: Aldbrough St John,
orth Yorkshire.
parated from Aldbrough
Paul by a tributary of
e Tees, the green
xtends on both sides of
e river and served two
rmer manors.

having gardens which slope down to the river bank. Heighington has five acres of square green split up by paths and roads and with the Norman church of St Michael and All Angels in the middle, in a fairly tight layout which surely cannot ever have had a real defensive function, in spite of the fact that access to the village centre was only at the corners of the square and could be closed by gates between the houses, some of which have now encroached on the original square plan.

Passing briefly into Cleveland before dealing with the western half of Durham, we may notice Egglescliffe, Norton and Greatham, all ancient villages now almost totally immersed in the depths of Tees-side industry. Egglescliffe manages to retain a semblance of semi-rural serenity round its rectangular green, shaded by maple trees and with the churchyard set back from it, with a view over the river from its position on high ground. This village centre only four miles from the centre of Stockton-on-Tees is preserved only by the fortunate absence of a through road, but Norton is not so lucky, being now totally enveloped by the industrial spread of Stockton. A main road runs through the old green with a traffic island in the middle, and one would hardly mention this former village at all if it were not that it still

ght: Gainford, Durham.
e of the best examples
he large greens
aracteristic of Durham,
th a vaguely
tangular shape lying
side a busy main road,
completely enclosed by
uses.

151

has stylish Georgian houses round it, which makes it the favoured residential area for Stockton's executives that it was when it could truly be called a rural village green. Yet it is still undeniably attractive and, though large, of more irregular shape than most Durham greens. Its impressive church of Saxon origin stands close by, with an eighteenth-century vicarage among the houses round the green.

Wolviston is another village now seemingly caught up in the net of roads cast out from the centre of Stockton, but it, too, retains its characteristic Durham green, spacious amid the buildings around it, which include not only the former manor house and manor farm but school, rectory and almshouses as well, all fine Georgian buildings such as one comes to expect in these parts.

Greatham is closer to Hartlepool – an even more daunting prospect to the average tourist seeking rural scenes, but it has a smaller green than the average in Durham, and again is made visually appealing by the attractive houses round it.

Before passing back inside the borders of the new County Durham, two greens in Tyne & Wear deserve brief mention. One is at Whitburn, on the coast north of Sunderland. The acre and a half of green here is not one of those modern amenities so often created in seaside resort developments, but an old and attractive tree-lined green with at least one house on it which dates back to the early seventeenth century. Houses on one side are elevated above the level of the green on a terrace, and the church tower peeps over the roofs on the south side.

Much more surprising is the green at Wallsend, originally a settlement on the Tyne at the eastern extremity of Hadrian's Wall and now an industrial appendage of Newcastle, with shipyards and coal transportation overwhelmingly in evidence. But the old part of the town retains its former village green in the face of all probabilities, though it had to fight to do so in the nineteenth century when the green was threatened by development.

Back in Durham, Easington and Trimdon are both mining villages where one would scarcely expect to find such relatively undisturbed features of rural England surviving the onslaught of industry, but Durham is more protective of its heritage than the Midlands in this respect, and both places have large greens, Easington's covering eight acres and Trimdon's having the church set in an island churchyard on it.

Lanchester's parish church of All Saints, which Pevsner called one of the most rewarding in the county, overlooks a wide green which is lined with the good-looking buildings we have by now come to expect in these parts and which we find once again at Witton-le-Wear to the south, with the village inn and a Methodist chapel on the green together with the former manor house, and other houses up the hillside overlooking it.

Hamsterley has a typical large rectangular green, well separated from the village church and nearly ten acres in extent. Across the River Wear, West Auckland also has interesting buildings along the edge of a large green, including the gabled Tudor hall and some seventeenth-century houses, while Staindrop's long green is roughly rectangular but narrows towards the end where the church stands.

Romaldkirk was one of Durham's prettiest acquisitions from Yorkshire's North Riding in the local government shuffle of the seventies, and one cannot improve on Pevsner's description of its green as 'eddying out in a variety of directions'. It is thus uncharacteristic of Durham, and what is more, its houses are of stone, have a certain uniformity of style and are scattered about instead of being arranged in straight rows. The Rose and Crown Inn is among them, and the informal look of this green village serves to emphasize the distinctive local pattern prevailing in old Durham, which we shall not find exactly repeated in Northumberland, so that we cannot ascribe Durham's individuality to any single northern influence. It is notice-

[caption, left margin:] ...ton-le-Wear, Durham. ...steeply sloping green ...is accompanied by ...or house, inn and ...hodist chapel, as well ...ore modern buildings.

able, however, that most of Durham's greens follow the national pattern in being in the lowland villages of the east rather than in the county's moorland villages. One interesting idea about the size of greens in Durham is that they have been enlarged as a result of removing dwellings erected by squatters.

Some Northumberland greens are surrounded by farm buildings and houses and can be seen as livestock pounds, but hardly as defensive layouts, and many of them are tiny by comparison with Durham's large areas. The greens here are generally quite clearly the original centres of nucleated villages, rather than the long greens in street villages we have seen in Durham. But there is a certain amount of overlapping style in the border regions, and it is only when we move northward through Northumberland that the difference becomes marked.

Wark and Simonburn, in the Tyne valley on the north side of Hadrian's Wall, were in Scotland in medieval times, and a great deal of border fighting occurred in the area, so that when we see the two greens of formal shape surrounded by houses and cottages, it is easy to see why the idea of the defensive closed village

Hamsterley, Durham. green is larger and rougher than the classi Durham type and was of the common land carved out of the medie Pennine forest.

154

ndrop, Durham. A
n of fairly regular and
cal shape and size for
area.

arose, but the protection of livestock from border raiders is the most that could have been achieved here, and that with some difficulty. Simonburn, in any case, was largely rebuilt in the eighteenth century, though the layout of the village, whose origins do not apparently go back beyond the Norman Conquest, was not drastically changed. Nightly watches were established in many border villages in the sixteenth century to guard livestock against red-haired Caledonian bandits.

Stamfordham, to the east, has a very long, sloping green with houses along both sides in a mixture of styles and materials – both brick and the dark northern stone – with an eighteenth-century village cross presented by the Swinburnes, who lorded it over this district for four hundred years. Another building on the green is the village lock-up, and there are also some fine chestnut trees.

At Whalton, the green is the scene of an annual bonfire, not on 5 November but on 4 July, with origins much more ancient than the American Independence Day celebrations. The date is the old Midsummer Eve, the independent villagers here having scorned the change in 1752 to the Gregorian calendar. They continued

Elsdon, Northumberla[nd]
A peaceful green now,
once was the scene of
skirmishes when Scott[ish]
raiders harried the bor[der]
villages.

to hold the ceremony on the same date and in the same place as they had for centuries before. The Bale Fire is a relic of an ancient pagan ritual in honour of the sun, and children dance round it in the twilight, when there is Morris dancing too.

Kirkwhelpington is an example of a village which has lost its green. Before the end of the eighteenth century, there was a fine circular green here, but the Duke of Somerset split it up into allotments for his village tenants.

Cambo, nearby, is a model village built of stone by the Blacketts of Wallington Hall originally, and continued by their successors as lords of the manor, the Trevelyans, and it was Sir Charles Trevelyan who created the central green there. Elsdon, on the other hand, has an old and unusually spacious green of over seven

156

acres, roughly triangular in shape, with roads crossing it and the church, former parsonage and one existing and another former inn among the buildings round it. This was once the capital of the Middle Marches, with a Norman motte-and-bailey castle, and the parsonage was one of those fortified northern houses called pele towers, where livestock could be secreted indoors on the ground floor when danger threatened; yet there can be no suggestion that Elsdon's green had a defensive function. There is an old pinfold in one corner, and farm animals were undoubtedly brought in for the night to be safe from marauding wolves or Scots. The former inn that is now a private house was called 'The Bacchus'; the one still in business is the 'Bird in Bush'.

Rothbury is a market town, but the triangular green on a steep slope beside the River Coquet where the original settlement grew up is still at the centre of its shops and houses, with the church at one corner, while Whittingham looks stylish for these parts, with stone houses roofed in grey slate or red pantiles about its well-kept greens which sport lime and sycamore trees, and as well as the village inn and shop there is, nearby, a former pele tower which was converted into almshouses for poor women in 1845.

To the north-east, Rock is another estate village, with the school building separating the green into two parts, but signs of the old settlement are still there, with the millpond, church, pele tower and old farm buildings.

The mighty rebuilt castle dominates the scene at Bamburgh, where a triangular green surrounded by small stone houses and known as 'The Grove' sits at the centre of what ought to be either a great town or a raucous seaside resort but is actually a remarkably peaceful and sedate coastal village. Bamburgh was once the capital of Northumbria and is now a holiday resort, but the Armstrong lords of the manor have preserved its country village atmosphere, and beside the green is the cottage where the young heroine Grace Darling died.

Right up on the Scottish border is Norham, with another impressively sited castle, though this one, high above the River Tweed, is in ruins. It was one of Turner's favourite subjects, and the painter obviously knew the village's main green well enough. It is again triangular and has a market cross on it with a weather-vane on top in the form of a fish, for the village economy used to depend on salmon fishing. The village green and church were at the centre of the original settlement but are now at one side, with the castle at the other, the two having become linked by development along what is now the main street, turning what was a nucleated village into a linear one.

— VIII —

The North West

CUMBRIA AND LANCASHIRE,
GREATER MANCHESTER AND MERSEYSIDE, CHESHIRE

The village greens of Cumbria might seem at first sight to defy the generalizations made in the first chapter. Firstly, as there are quite a few of them, they seem to contradict the assertion that greens are mostly concentrated on the eastern side of England. Secondly, as everyone knows that Cumbria is sheep-farming country, they challenge the assumption that greens are found chiefly in arable farming villages. And thirdly, the style of some of the greens raises the question once again of the true origin of the green village.

The first two points can be dealt with fairly easily. The concentration of village greens in Cumbria is not in the Lake District or the western coastal region but in the north and along the eastern border of the county, adjacent to the Northumberland, Durham and Yorkshire borders, in the lowlands where there is mixed arable and pastoral farming. Although there are small greens at such as Elterwater and Stonethwaite, greens in the Lake District villages are few and far between.

The third argument is, of course, more tricky. There is a terrific variety in the size, shape and style of Cumbria's greens, and it will perhaps be wise to plunge in at the deep end and deal with the green at Milburn, which has already been discussed briefly in the first chapter. If there is one green in England which lends itself more than any other to the evidence in support of defensive strategy, this is it, and we ought to consider it carefully. I have already described how the buildings are arranged tightly round the strictly rectangular green, which is $4\frac{1}{2}$ acres in extent and split up by paths and roadways. As we enter the village centre from the south-west corner of the green, we pass a Wesleyan chapel built in 1834 and facing up the green towards the Victorian school building at the other end. The school is the only building which is actually *on* the green, being on a kind of triangular island site with roads all round it. Half-way up the green, which has some trees on it, is a tall, permanent maypole, on the northern side, with a weathercock at the top. Round the green, nearly forty groups of buildings or detached houses and barns stand in tight formation, facing inward and with only narrow gaps between them. The green can only be entered at the four corners of the rectangle, and the roads out from the north-east and south-east corners lead nowhere, those at the western end linking up with a road connecting Milburn with other Pennine settlements to north and south. The church is well outside this village nucleus, to the south-west. It was there early in the thirteenth century. The lord of the manor's house, Howgill Castle, is even further from the village centre, higher up the fellside to the east, and dates originally from the fourteenth century.

One of the problems with interpreting the meaning of Milburn's layout is that the church and the fortified house are the only two really old buildings there are. Around the green, there is nothing earlier than the seventeenth century, and most houses are of the eighteenth and nineteenth centuries. So how do we know that the village plan conforms to the original one and is not merely a development during the years of border troubles with the Scots, when mosstroopers from country with poor soil would raid richer lands to the south and steal cattle and horses? The name of the village is Anglo-Saxon. 'Burn' was old English for a stream or brook, and what is now called Milburn Beck, with its tautological Scandinavian suffix, flows south of the village, nearer to the church than the green. The maypole on the green, meanwhile, is set into the base of an old village cross. Outside the village centre, traces of medieval open fields can be seen in the long and narrow shapes of the modern fields, and the roads to other villages link Milburn with a string of nucleated villages reaching north-south along the lower slopes of the Pennines. Milburn therefore represents a distinct settlement pattern in these parts, and there can be little doubt that the modern village plan has been inherited from the invaders from northern Europe who came here after the departure of the Romans and established their own familiar village patterns, possibly with each peasant house having some geographical relation to the strips in the open fields, as in the Danish *solskifte*.

The argument that such villages were designed for defence surely ignores the savage realities of naked aggression, and the fact that, in all such examples of supposedly defensive villages, the houses face inwards surely ruins the theory. You did not turn your back to the enemy, and whether you did or not, there was nothing to prevent the attackers burning and advancing from the backs of what were then, after all, only flimsy buildings of timber and thatch.

It seems almost self-evident that, in villages where arable farming was the predominant occupation, greens such as Milburn's were designed to contain livestock. The closing of the gaps between houses would prevent sheep or cattle

Milburn, Cumbria. The
classic 'defensive' green,
showing the maypole, the
school on the green, and
houses closely grouped
round it.

wandering off (we use cattle grids for that purpose today). It would also afford some limited protection from marauding wolves, and when the access roads were closed, as they probably were at night, the green became a large pound. At Badby in Northamptonshire, where we found a large, irregular green at the village centre, there is another green beside the main road, called Pinfold Green, and many other names here and there throughout Britain attest to the importance of various greens as livestock enclosures.

Dufton is not far from Milburn, and here the green is also rectangular and of very similar size to Milburn's, but more open, and though it is surrounded by cottages and farm buildings, there is nothing obviously protective about it. There is an avenue of trees down the middle, and Dufton Pike rises above its rooftops on one side, but the most notable thing about Dufton's green is the parish pump, a striking stone structure with a ball finial at the top, all painted in that curious maroon colour which, for some unexplained reason, is very popular in the Pennine region.

Temple Sowerby's green is small compared with those at Milburn and Dufton, and split up by the scattering of roads and houses round it, but the village is an attractive place that belonged to the Knights Templars once and has a quite different and less formal nature than its neighbours. Some of the houses have granite cobbles set into their walls for decorative effect.

Over to the west, on the fringes of the Lake District, Askham and Lowther have greens of sorts, though neither place corresponds with the traditional image of a green village in this area. Askham's green is of fair size, but more like those we found in Yorkshire, with houses stretched out along both sides of its sloping length and with a road junction in the middle. The houses and cottages are in Lake District white with the Queen's Head among them. From the top end of the village, the ruin of the Lowther family's mock Gothic castle can be seen, and the Lowthers, who ruled vast territories in Cumbria and became earls of Lonsdale, destroyed at least one village in creating their house and park, rebuilding Lowther in a less inconvenient spot. The new village of Lowther is a formal affair for the estate workers with a small green of half an acre and a pump on a path in the middle, with houses enclosing it on three sides, but it all dates only from the early nineteenth century. Greystoke's green has the Boot and Shoe Inn facing the entrance to the local big-shot's place, Greystoke Castle, a medieval castle practically rebuilt in the nineteenth century in Tudor style.

There are a few small greens in the Lake District itself, but none of them of much significance. Coniston has one bearing a memorial plaque to Donald Campbell, who was killed attempting to break the water-speed record on Coniston Water, and the churchyard is close by, containing the grave of John Ruskin. Elterwater has a small green with the inn beside it. at the centre of a small quarrying village now overrun by tourists, but a delightful study in vernacular architecture, with cottages built of local slate rubble.

Farther north, Caldbeck and Hesket Newmarket are close neighbours with differing views on what a village green should look like. Caldbeck's is a rambling nine-acre job of rough grass with a duckpond and quite unprepossessing, known to visitors who come to see the grave of huntsman John Peel in the churchyard. Near the south corner of the green are some big farm gates through which a path is signposted to 'The Howk' – an eerie limestone gorge with the ruins of a bobbin-mill and a swallowhole known as 'the Fairies' Kettle'. The Norsemen left a folklore in this region replete with tales of 'little folk' – fairies, elves, goblins, pixies and so forth, who no doubt still dance on village greens at night when ordinary folk are in bed.

The green at Hesket Newmarket is quiet enough for them now, though once the place was a busy market town, where Dickens and his friend Wilkie Collins stayed once. An eighteenth-century market cross stands on the green, which is smaller than Caldbeck's (five acres) and quite unlike it, being a wide strip of grass up the middle of the village street, again like the greens common in Yorkshire, with houses along both sides. Nowadays, of course, there are too many parked cars and wires around to give the impression of rural serenity the village ought to convey.

Near Carlisle, Dalston and Wetheral likewise present contrasts in village green styles, Dalston's being big, with houses and church clustered round it, and Wetheral's triangular and more formal with a market cross on it and a road from one corner leading to the bank of the River Eden. This is a well-kept green in an attractive sandstone village, but unfortunately the green is dominated by Victorian buildings out of character with the vernacular style, in yellowish brick or cement rendering.

Right over in the east, near the border with Durham, is Garrigill, on the upper reaches of the South Tyne as it descends from Alston Moor. It is a small place, undisturbed by tourists, with houses, shop, church and Congregational chapel round a small green, all dating from the eighteenth century, when Quaker mining magnates came here to exploit the moor's lead deposits and built or extended villages for their employees. Garrigill's dark buildings of grey stone are well preserved in their sheltered valley, and the green lends the village a look of calm and prosperity compared with the exposed and ravaged settlements out on the bleak moorland. The village name, of Norse origin, indicates that there was a settlement here before the lead-miners came in force, and as we return to the sandstone villages of the Eden valley, we find a whole string of villages that have the Scandinavian '–by' name ending, many of them having greens at their centres, as if they were of Anglo-Saxon foundation and merely developed or taken over by the Norsemen.

Melmerby and Gamblesby are among them, with greens of startling contrast in size – Gamblesby's a small thing with some sandstone still in evidence in the buildings round it, while Melmerby has a broad eleven-acre green with a beck flowing through it, and buildings around it which only rarely show the local stone in their walls.

Farther south, beyond the villages round Milburn, where we came in, Orton and Ravenstonedale have a few small patches of green between them and are attractive and interesting old villages, while Soulby has a three-acre green, and Milnthorpe, near Cumbria's border with Lancashire, has its church on the small green with an eighteenth-century market cross nearby. On the Furness peninsula, trees fringe the attractive green at Lindal.

What emerges from looking at Cumbria's greens in isolation is that there is no predominant local pattern, and it seems most likely that the so-called defensive style of Milburn's green is explained by the tribal customs of the particular wanderers who came here and established the settlement in the first place. If it were a village plan imposed by later landowners, such as the powerful ecclesiastical houses, and it seemed such a good and necessary idea at the time, it is difficult to understand why more greens in the region do not conform to it, and it is surely more reasonable to ascribe such greens to a particular group of settlers at a particular point in history.

Dufton, Cumbria. An attractive village centre standing on high ground with Pennine views beyond, and the village pump on the green.

Temple Sowerby, Cumbria. A nice northern green which slopes steeply to one side, formerly a property of the Knights Templars.

Melmerby, Cumbria. A rough area of eleven acres of grassland in one of a line of villages on the western fringes of the Pennines.

Slaidburn, Lancashire.
The village's green slopes
up from the river bank a
has the 'courthouse' inn
Hark to Bounty, nearby.

It is not really any more surprising that the pattern of village greens should change from time to time and place to place, even in a small area, than that an up-to-date shopping centre built twenty years ago along a town thoroughfare should already seem old-fashioned compared with a more recent covered-in pedestrian precinct.

One or two of Lancashire's present village greens were acquired from Yorkshire's former West Riding through the Local Government Act of the seventies, so we should not be surprised to find the long green of indeterminate shape with houses along both sides, but neither Slaidburn nor Bolton-by-Bowland conforms strictly to this local pattern. Slaidburn's green is triangular and, so far from being stretched along the main street, is at the bottom end of the village near the river, with plenty of trees and stone walls round it. Offenders against the laws of the royal Forest of Bowland would have known this green well enough, for Slaidburn was the forest's medieval capital, and the court used to sit in an upper room of the village inn, called 'Hark to Bounty'. The name is supposed to have been taken from a former parson's dog which enjoyed, as it were, benefit of clergy, for other dogs which barked during divine service were disciplined with whips still to be seen in the church, but a similar noise from the parson's dog merely elicited the sycophantic exclamation 'Hark to Bounty.' So daft a story is probably true. Such licence was not extended to the Forest of Bowland's human felons, however, and when the judge passed sentence from his bench in the still-preserved courtroom in the inn, it must often have been to the village green where the miserable guilty party was removed, to sit in the stocks for a minor offence or to be whipped for a more serious one, if indeed he was not actually hanged for poaching.

Bolton-by-Bowland still has its stocks on one of the greens, for there are two here, the one with the stocks also having the remains of a market cross. Grey stone and whitewashed cottages are scattered about fairly haphazardly, with the Rose and Crown nearby, while the church and school stand above the higher green. This quiet village is in Ribblesdale, sandwiched between Bowland Forest on the north side and the whale-backed Pendle Hill on the south, and on the other side of the river is Downham, often called Lancashire's prettiest village.

A tributary stream of the Ribble trickles through Downham's lower green, crossed by a stone road bridge near which children vie with the local ducks for paddling space, but the stocks are preserved here, too, and the greens are in a well-kept village of stone walls, houses and farm buildings over which the Assheton family have held sway for centuries, becoming involved unwontedly in the story of Pendle's notorious Lancashire Witches, for the then lord of the manor, Richard Assheton, was supposedly the victim of one of the evil women's spells. The ancestral home, Downham Hall, stands with the church and the public house (the Assheton Arms naturally) on the higher green where the stocks are to be found.

Superstition has survived much of the modern onslaught of materialism in Lancashire, and on one of the two greens at Inglewhite the old market cross is surmounted by a stone figure of a 'Green Man', after which one of the village pubs was named. The Green Man, or Jack-in-the-Green, was a figure clothed in oak leaves who represented the spirit of the forest in pagan May Day celebrations and was associated as a fertility symbol with ritual dramas performed by Morris dancers. What is more memorable about Inglewhite's green is that it was the site of a sheep and cattle fair which made it a hubbub of activity for a few days each year when farmers came from far and wide to do profitable deals in livestock and exchange gossip in the three pubs the village had in those days.

Wrea Green's five acres is large for Lancashire, and the older part of Lytham St Anne's has a village green near the seashore with a windmill on it. Rivington, however, was almost sunk beneath the waters of a new reservoir created for Liverpool's benefit in the nineteenth century, but it retains a small triangular green with an early Unitarian chapel on it – built during the reign of Queen Anne – and a set of stocks behind the wall of the vicarage. Some cottages stand on the site of a mill that was working here in the reign of Elizabeth I, but this attractive village near the outskirts of Bolton has been invaded by bigger industrialists in the present century – Levers and Pilkingtons have had their homes here – and the M61 motorway roars past on the other side of the reservoir. Nevertheless, the nearby hamlet of White Coppice also has a green – somewhat larger, with the village cricket pitch on it – and Newburgh, over to the west, sports a market cross on its triangular green, within an ace of the new industrial town of Skelmersdale.

Bolton-by-Bowland, Lancashire. Stocks rema[...] by the old village cross [...] this small triangular gre[...] in Ribblesdale.

Downham, Lancashire. This pretty stone village[...] a noted beauty spot by t[...] riverside and has anothe[...] of the country's threatened school buildings close to its gre[...]

Among the great industrial conurbations of south Lancashire, many villages with give-away 'green' names are tucked away, such as Hindley Green, Haughton Green and Astley Green, which once had rural open areas serving their parishes in the traditional way before the Industrial Revolution came along with King Cotton to reign over the district. Yet even in Merseyside and Greater Manchester, the occasional old green can still be found, like a triangular warning sign against too much interference with rural tradition. Chorlton-cum-Hardy may have lost its old green in its swallowing up by Manchester, but Worsley, beyond the Coronation Street side of the great build-up, hangs on to two small greens, Roe Green and Beesley Green, more surprisingly in view of the Duke of Bridgewater's coal-mining and canal-digging activities there in the eighteenth century.

Ainsdale, just outside Southport, stretches westward as a coastal resort now but still has a triangular green at its old centre, with the village war memorial on it and some old cottages around.

Thornton Hough ought not to be overlooked in this review of village greens. This Merseyside village is on the Wirral and formerly belonged to Cheshire. It has church, manor house, vicarage, shop and smithy with a spreading chestnut tree, and sounds like a perfect English village of old but is in fact a sort of country cousin of Port Sunlight, created largely by Lord Leverhulme as an estate village on the earlier development of Joseph Hirst, who had a fifth clock face added to the Victorian church tower he had built in 1867, because he found he could not see the time from the windows of his house. The church looks over the large green with a pavilion on it, beside which are estate cottages in a pleasing mixture of styles, with half-timbering, Dutch-style gables, ornamental brick chimneys and so on. Although the green at Thornton Hough is a fake in the sense that it is a modern creation masquerading as an 'olde worlde' green, it is at the same time in the genuine rural tradition in being a recreational area for the communal use of the residents.

Another modern green was planned for Woodchurch (now part of Birkenhead) after the Second World War, but this never materialized, although the village lost its original green in the development programme, unlike Heswall, slightly safer on the Dee side of the peninsula, which still has its four-acre green known as 'The Puddydale'.

As we move southward into Cheshire, the incidence of village greens declines rapidly. There are greens remaining in urban areas with becoming names like Paradise Green at Knutsford and Hawk Green at Marple. But apart from a little string of green villages stretching south-eastward from Knutsford – Lower Peover, Goostrey, Twemlow and Astbury – Cheshire has little to offer us, and we must begin

to acknowledge that scarcity of greens down the western half of England remarked on in the first chapter.

Lower Peover's green has the village sign on it and cottages around, but the church, inn and village school are some distance away in a sort of conspiratorial huddle, as if they wished to have nothing to do with the green end of the place, the name of which is pronounced 'Peever' and sometimes 'Peever Inferior', which may explain the stand-offishness! Astbury's church, one of the most interesting in the county, is closer to the centre, where there are again brick cottages round a small triangular green.

Christleton is now a suburb of Chester, just outside the ring road on the east side, but it has one of the best of the county's few greens, an area of $2\frac{1}{2}$ acres shaded by trees, with some half-timbered Victorian almshouses beside the pond and the Ring o' Bells inn nearby.

Why is there such a dramatic difference in the pattern of settlement between the western Pennines and the country south of the Mersey? The answer lies partly with the Norman Conquest. The region of Cumbria and the Welsh Marches had been only sparsely settled by British and Anglo-Saxon farmers, the latter establishing a few scattered villages and hamlets centred on greens in country where the predominant pattern was – and still is up to a point – of remote hamlets and isolated farms. William II aimed at greater colonization of this thinly populated area after his conquest of the north, and as the Anglo-Saxon Chronicle records, he sent 'very many peasants' southwards from Carlisle 'with their wives and livestock to settle there and till the soil'. They established villages in the north-west which were usually linear rather than nucleated, but settlement in the Welsh Marches remained sparse and scattered, and neither Anglian nor Norman village patterns radically changed the kind of settlement which remained from prehistoric and Roman times.

The odd thing about the large greens of northern England, in Yorkshire, Durham and Cumbria especially, is that they occur in upland country where there is wealth of common land, whereas in other parts of England the number of greens seems almost in inverse proportion to the amount of common land in each county. This has to be explained either by settlement at a different period or by settlement by different people, and the latter seems the most obvious explanation. The large rectangular greens totally enclosed by houses suggest settlement by pioneers with a different idea of social organization from those who created the small triangular greens farther south.

Village Greens
of the West Midlands

DERBYSHIRE, STAFFORDSHIRE, SHROPSHIRE, HEREFORD & WORCESTER, WEST MIDLANDS, WARWICKSHIRE AND GLOUCESTERSHIRE

Proceeding through the other Welsh border counties from Cheshire, we find unarguable confirmation of the scarcity of green villages in the western part of England. In Staffordshire, Shropshire and Hereford & Worcester, there are hardly any greens at all, and even those that do occur are of no more than pocket-handkerchief size. But if we take the west Midlands as a whole, the picture is slightly rosier, because Derbyshire and Warwickshire, forming an hour-glass shape in the middle of England, have a respectable number of greens to show between them, and the Gloucestershire Cotswolds also help to make up the numbers in this region.

Derbyshire's greens are scattered throughout the county, from the Peak District in the north to the industrial lowlands in the south, and the chief characteristic they nearly all share is their small size. Most of Derbyshire's greens are less than half an acre in extent, but they offer much contrast in appearance and significance.

That at Castleton, in the Peak District, almost fades into inconsequence by comparison with that village's dramatic surroundings such as Peveril Castle, Peak Cavern and Mam Tor, but the green at Tissington, to the south, is one of the chief features that earns the village the reputation as one of the county's prettiest. This green is triangular and has the church, manor house, vicarage and a few attractive houses of pale limestone set back from it, with trees around and upon it, and the Yewtree Well nearby – one of the five village wells which are dressed on Ascension Day each year with designs on Biblical themes, made with flowers. This annual ceremony, deriving, according to tradition, from the fact that Tissington's wells have protected the villagers from drought and disease by always supplying pure water, is what draws most visitors here, but the beauty of this village is more easily appreciated at quieter times, when the green stands at the centre of a serene place with no main road through it, and the autumn sunlight picks out the yellow lichen on the garden walls and the dazzling Virginia creeper on the walls of the Jacobean Tissington Hall, seat of the Fitzherbert family to whom the village owes its careful preservation. Some might complain that the preservation went too far. There is no traditional village pub near the centre, and the approach road from the east is via what is humorously described on a signpost as a 'ford', although after heavy rain you could sink a bus in it.

Between Castleton and Tissington there is an arc of green villages – Litton, Edensor and Winster – of which Winster's is the largest, but as that place is a town owing its growth to lead-mining, we will not dwell on it. Litton's green still has the old stocks, standing outside the Red Lion in a village which, like Tissington, dresses its well with floral designs each year and has further signs of ancient custom in some walled fields outside the village. They are very narrow and of long reverse S shape. They are enclosed sections of the feudal open fields, and their shape is due to the ridge-and-furrow patterns made a thousand years ago by turning the teams of oxen at each end of the strips. The green at Edensor is remarkable but not old, having been created as the nucleus of the new Chatsworth estate village in the nineteenth century, when the sixth Duke of Devonshire wished to have the old village obliterated from the view from his windows. The Duke's gardener, Joseph Paxton, and a Derby architect, John Robertson, planned the new village around a spacious green and planted laburnum trees on it, with the village church above and the estate workers' houses spread out around it in a variety of styles, but all built of the local Millstone Grit. The old inn, whose one-time jolly landlord had won the approval of James Boswell, survived the demolition job along with the basic fabric of the church. Brassington belonged to this little group of villages not so long ago, but characteristically of the industrial villages, it has turned its village green into a car-park.

Over to the east, Elmton and North Wingfield keep up the even distribution of green villages through Derbyshire, though here there is a contrast in size, North Wingfield's green being a typical half acre, whereas Elmton has a green which, at three acres, is quite large for this county.

Ockbrook, in south Derbyshire, still has a green which used to be at the centre of a Moravian settlement founded here in 1750. The chapel and some brick cottages join hands around the green, so to speak, with Georgian houses which were eventually converted into a school for girls.

On the other side of Derby, the greens at Etwall and Dalbury are dutifully diminutive, but the latter's green is, strictly speaking, in the part of the parish charmingly called Dalbury-with-Less, though it actually has more in this particular respect than both its immediate neighbour and Etwall.

Norton-in-Hales, Shropshire. Behind the seat on this small triangular green is the so-called Bradling Stone.

Little Barrington, Gloucestershire. This is a large Cotswold green with attractive groups of stone cottages scattered around it.

orth Bovey, Devon. The
nnual village fête on the
een known as the
laystow'

At the southern tip of Derbyshire, where the sand runs through the narrow waist of the hour-glass into Warwickshire, Lullington, Netherseal and Coton-in-the-Elms manage to muster about half an acre of green between the three of them but help to save the green village from disappearing altogether in the west Midlands, which is more than can be said for the villages of Staffordshire, despite the sprinkling of enticing 'green' names here and there – Pye Green, Burntwood Green, Butters Green. Longdon, on the north side of Cannock Chase, has a green of fair size with some attractive houses set round it, and there is a small green at Trysull, near Wolverhampton, where Samuel Johnson visited a resident aunt.

Shropshire, alas, is even more devoid of nucleated green villages, its chief saving grace being the tiny triangular green at Norton-in-Hales, where a large sandstone boulder behind a wooden seat is known as the Bradling Stone. The tradition is that any man or boy found working in this village after noon on Shrove Tuesday used to be unceremoniously bumped or 'bradled' on this rock to teach him a lesson, and I dare say this local custom could be called an early demonstration of union solidarity. The green stands in front of the village church and has naturally helped Norton-in-Hales to its past success in the Best Kept Village competition in this county.

Albrighton, Upton Magna and Preston-upon-the-Weald-Moors, all in the east of Shropshire, where there is significantly little common land in a county generally well endowed with it, still have small greens, but in the south and west green villages are virtually non-existent, with the distinguished exception of Minton, at the foot of the Long Mynd near Church Stretton, where stone cottages surround a not specially attractive green in a village of Saxon origin with the remains of a motte-and-bailey castle nearby.

The county of Hereford & Worcester emphasizes the dearth of green villages in the Welsh Marches, where the settlement pattern has been of scattered and isolated farmsteads and hamlets rather than nucleated settlements. Here, of all places, one would expect village greens to be abundant if their real purpose was to give communities some security against attack from outside. Would not Anglo-Saxon or Norman settlers have imposed this pattern on the Celtic fringe of the west if the village green was seen as a piece of defensive strategy? But if the green was to provide a reserve for livestock, what need of it in this area, which is chiefly concerned with pastoral farming anyway and in which the clearing of forest was done in the first place to accommodate livestock rather than grow crops?

Herefordshire has a modest cluster of very tiny greens near the Welsh border around Moccas, at places such as Dorstone, Blakemere and Preston-on-Wye. The one at Dorstone is a small, triangular green on a raised level with the village shop

Litton, Derbyshire. The green in this attractive village is ideal for summe customers of the Red Lio Stocks and market cross remain nearby.

and post office among the tightly packed buildings around it in an otherwise rather scattered village. On the green is a square stone housing for the village pump, now with a tap in it and with a seat built round it.

Withington, near Hereford, is an appealing village with its church and houses set round a green, and over to the east, flanking the border between the two former counties, are Cradly on one side and Hanley Swan on the other, both with the small greens characteristic of this region. We find similar small patches of grass at Suckley and Powick, Hallow and Martin Hussingtree, Feckenham, Inkberrow and Clifton-on-Teme, but it is not until we reach the southern extremity of Worcestershire that we may feel compelled to pause over one or two greens of less ordinariness.

Cleeve Prior's triangular green has some nice stone-built cottages round it, and the green at Broadway only fades into relative insignificance by comparison with the other multitudinous attractions of that spectacular stone village. If the green at Broadway were not surrounded by some of the most interesting stone building in the county, it would call for much more attention in its own right, but it requires a peculiarly single-minded fellow to deal with this little green in isolation from its beautiful and alluring surroundings. Henry James and Edmund Gosse were among those who knew this green and helped to make the village famous.

Ripple has an attractive green with manor house and almshouses nearby, not to mention the village's fine twelfth-century church, and its village stocks carefully preserved. But Worcestershire's biggest surprise lies in wait for us at Bushley, for here, after the little green triangles we have become used to, there is a comparatively

ensor, Derbyshire. The
urch rebuilt by Sir
eorge Gilbert Scott in
867 dominates the green
eated in this model
llage thirty years earlier.

massive-looking green of fourteen acres. We should not expect many greens of this size anywhere in the Midlands.

In the idiotically named West Midlands county (idiotic because we cannot now refer to the west Midlands as a region without making it clear which we are talking about), there are naturally few village greens left in an area almost totally occupied by Birmingham, Wolverhampton, Coventry and their industrial satellites, and the temptation is to ignore this unappealing bit of England and pass on quickly. But oddly enough, the new county possesses a couple of greens well worth notice, and one which cannot possibly be left out.

Meriden, West Midlands
The prettified base and shaft of a medieval cross on this triangular green are claimed to stand at the very centre of England.

It will hardly surprise anyone to learn that the greens of West Midlands county are situated in that little area of breathing space that occurs between the build-up of Coventry and that of Solihull, but one green worth remarking on is now within Birmingham itself, at Kings Norton – one of those former village greens that have survived being swallowed up, like Jonah, by the whale of a city. One can still appreciate the village character of the place with the sloping, triangular green closely accompanied by the parish church and the Saracen's Head Inn among other nearby buildings. As with other urban greens, such as Paddington in London and Seacroft in Leeds, the survival of this one seems like a sort of minor miracle. Several Birmingham suburbs retain their green names, like those in London we noticed. Here are Winson Green, Lyndon Green, Wells Green, Hall Green and Acock's Green, among others, but there is little sign of old village centres in these places, whilst Bournville's indisputably well-preserved green is, of course, a modern creation.

Berkswell, near Coventry, has a small triangular green with seats and four trees on it, as well as the village stocks and whipping post which are fenced in to make them, if possible, even more of an eyesore than they were before. Presumably this has been done to protect the old instruments of justice from damage by vandals. It was the people who were put in the stocks who needed protection from the rabble in the old days, but they never got it. Now the stocks themselves are protected as if they are the pride of the community. They have five holes. No doubt there was a one-legged village idiot who was confidently expected to be a regular tenant when the contraption was being made by the village carpenter. Certainly the villagers were zealous in their pursuit of malefactors, for they had their own Association for the Prosecution of Felons before there was a regular police force, and, like the redundant stocks themselves, the association survives. The village shop and almshouses are of the company that surround the green.

The West Midlands green which we cannot on any account ignore is the one at Meriden, if only because of its claim to be at the very centre of England. I have never been able to grasp how this extraordinary statistic can be computed, but the proud claim is there for all to see, nevertheless: a headless medieval cross with an octagonal shaft on the well-kept green, which is in the shape of a long triangle with its short side rounded, and fringed by houses, shops and telephone exchange. The cross has a low fence round it to protect and dignify this sacred cow of a landmark, and at the point of the green there is a memorial to cyclists who died in both world wars, Meriden being a sort of holy city for cyclists on account of its alleged central position. There is also a flagpole on the green, and it goes without saying that, in a place which depends for its fame on faith, this is often taken for a maypole.

Warwickshire has a good number of village greens, all more or less characteristic of the Midland counties in being small and triangular. That at Mancetter in the north is a triangular patch of grass with church, almshouses and cottages beside it, and the cemetery on another side, but this green no longer looks like the centre of anywhere, for Mancetter has gravitated towards Atherstone and become part of it, losing its separate identity to a large extent.

Farther south, Stoneleigh and Stretton-on-Dunsmore are typical of the region's green villages – the greens are tiny and apparently unloved. Stoneleigh has two, both triangular and both scruffy and unkempt. One has a bus shelter on it, and the other an ugly brick building of the nineteenth century, and the trees present do little to rescue the greens from the impression that, here in the no-nonsense

Below: Warmington, Warwickshire. The fairly spacious green among limestone cottages has one of the best of the rare Midland duckponds.

Midlands, village greens are a thing of the past and the sooner they are built over the better. There are some attractive and interesting buildings in the village, and these obviously account for Stoneleigh's reputation for being 'picturesque'.

Stretton-on-Dunsmore's green is a little better, though much of it consists merely of banks by the stream running through the village. One triangular patch with a tall tree and a seat built round it lies in front of an attractive half-timbered and gabled farmhouse, but there is not space enough for the village children to gather on it, let alone a few animals to graze it.

Dunchurch and Napton-on-the-Hill show some contrasts in style if not in size. This is largely due to their relative situations, Napton being off the main roads while Dunchurch is very definitely on them, and in consequence has litter bins and a telephone kiosk on its green, as well as the stocks, and Midland Bank, shops and brick houses round it, with one nice thatched cottage standing out from all the modern development.

Tanworth-in-Arden, on the opposite side of the county, has a small green round which the influence of modern Birmingham is not as strong as in the rest of this commuter village, and Aston Cantlow, to the south, which Shakespeare's parents are supposed to have come from, is still a fairly unspoiled village round its green nucleus.

As we move towards the southern end of Warwickshire, things get better. Welford-on-Avon has an attractive green with a maypole on it, lying off the main road through the village, and there are thatched houses and cottages around. One of the village's three inns is called 'The Shakespeare', and it is not difficult to imagine that the poet walked across this green in the Avon valley not far from Stratford. He would have seen the green and basic village plan, four hundred years ago, much as it is today.

He would have seen the green at Preston-on-Stour, too, no doubt, though this would have looked very different then, for brick has been used in the village buildings since Shakespeare's time, giving it a wholly different character from the poor country hovels of the sixteenth century.

Radway and Warmington are neighbours near the Oxfordshire border, the latter being the big brother as far as their greens are concerned. Radway's is very small, but Warmington's is considerably larger and has a large duckpond, with the gabled and mullioned Elizabethan manor house among the neat limestone cottages around it. The village looks a serene place today, but the churchyard contains the graves of soldiers who died in the Civil War, after Charles I had marched his army through this rural village and met his enemy at Edgehill, not half an hour's march to the west.

The Anglo-Saxon 'ton' ending gives us a group of three greens at Ilmington, Tredington and Honington. Only Tredington lies directly on a main road and consequently has more evidence of modern building than the others, but it was a nucleated green village at first like its neighbours. All three greens are roughly the same size, but Tredington's is fairly shapeless now and split up into bits and pieces.

Ilmington actually has two greens, Upper and Lower, and down-to-earth affairs like the village pub and cottages are beside the bottom green, naturally, while the larger top green basks in the company of church and manor house. The pub is

edington, Warwick-
re. One of a close trio
Anglo-Saxon villages,
s one is on a main
d and just manages to
ep its ancient green
re or less intact.

nington, Warwickshire.
is green, one of two in
village, seems more
cure, with the Howard
ns on one side and
age houses on the
er.

urton-on-the-Water,
ucestershire. Attractive
en the tourists are not
wded on it, the green is
both sides of the River
ndrush, with stone
dges matching the
estone shops and
uses.

the Howard Arms, and a senior citizen of the village told me that, sixty years ago, the landlady there used to wash out the beer barrels and sell the washing-up water to the locals at a halfpenny a pint. Honington has no pub or shop, doubtless because the lords of the manor, the Parker family of the magnificent seventeenth-century Honington Hall close by, did not want the working classes at their gates in drunken male or clacking female gatherings.

Sutton-under-Brailes and Whichford complete this brief picture of Warwickshire's green villages. The former is a secluded place with trees and stone cottages round its two-acre green, while Whichford, also well away from major roads, has a good size square and gently sloping green with the village school on it, built of ironstone, and an inn called the Norman Knight among the houses round it.

The Cotswold villages of Gloucestershire, unusually for western England, boast a modest crop of greens with much variety in their size and style, although generally they conform to Midland England's tendency towards smaller-than-average greens. The former communal green at Snowshill is a smallish area which has been taken over by the churchyard, since the village church was built in the middle of it, like the one at Hawkedon in Suffolk. But whereas Hawkedon's consecrated ground is confined, at Snowshill it has insinuated itself all over the green, which is now walled in. The mellow limestone houses round this green include the former manor house, once belonging to the abbot of Winchcombe, whose sheep grazed the surrounding hills, and now preserved as a museum by the National Trust since a latter-day lord of the manor, Charles Paget Wade, filled the place to overflowing with his collection of cuckoo clocks, penny-farthings and other curiosities.

Across country at Broadwell, the village houses gather round a green alongside the street, which is crossed by a tributary stream of the River Evenload, forming a shallow ford.

The green at Guiting Power is small, neat and attractive, with what looks like a medieval cross standing at its edge as well as the Farmer's Arms. The cross, however, is a modern war memorial designed like a medieval churchyard cross and is in keeping with a village whose well-kept stylishness qualifies it as one of the best greens in England, its grass neatly mown and surrounded by gabled stone houses with mullioned windows.

Several greens cluster together where the Cotswolds' tourist industry is most concentrated. Unquestionably the best known is at Bourton-on-the-Water, where the little River Windrush flows through the large green, crossed by attractive stone bridges. Unfortunately in the summer months this green might as well be Blackpool beach for all you can see of it, to such an extent that the village has been granted the dubious honour of double yellow lines in its streets and thus takes on the appear-

Lower Slaughter, Gloucestershire. The same river that waters Bourton flows through this delightful Cotswold green.

ance of a small town. But it is worth visiting Bourton in the winter to savour its attractions, with its charming shops and houses of local stone round a green enhanced by fine trees as well as the sparkling stream and its clapper bridges. One thing that is instantly obvious about Bourton's green, however, is that, although the village has Roman and Anglo-Saxon origins, this is a 'cultivated' green. It has been altered and developed with the same eye for commercial success that won the village the ludicrous nickname 'the Venice of the Cotswolds'. So although this green is among the beauties, it is not one on which to study the use and development of the traditional English green.

From that point of view, the green at Bledington, not far away, is more apt. This is an irregular green with a maypole on it and genuine old cottages tucked around it here and there, looking as if it has hardly changed in centuries. Bledington's Morris dancers had a wide reputation at one time, and the green was the regular scene of village May Day festivities.

Wyck Rissington and Great Rissington each have their greens, Great Rissington's being a triangular one on a hill at the top of the main street. Wyck Rissington's neighbour Lower Slaughter is more famous than itself – one of the gems among the Cotswold villages. A little tributary stream of the Windrush flows through this green and is crossed by several pretty stone bridges, as at Bourton, with Cotswold stone houses around. But unlike Bourton, Lower Slaughter does not look like a village with an eye on the main chance. Its green still gets packed with tourists in the summer months, but you can feel here that this green was laid out for the benefit of the villagers and not for the coach-trippers, and if only the grooves in the old stone walls could be made to give up their secrets like a gramophone record, they could tell us what goings-on there were on this green long before the Cotswolds were discovered by the tourist trade.

Farmington, to the south, is a quarrying village with a small green beside the main road bearing an octagonal gabled pumphouse on tall wooden legs. This was erected in 1898 at the expense of the village's namesake in Connecticut, which was then celebrating the tricentenary of its foundation.

Little Barrington, a little way east, has a larger green of triangular shape with, once again, a stream flowing through it. The stone-built houses are in terraces on two sides. One group of charming old cottages stands a little higher than the main part of the green behind a yew tree which itself suggests the antiquity of this attractive open space. There is nothing cultivated or pretentious about this lovely green.

Nearer Cirencester, the Ampney group of villages, in which the 'p' is silent, have a few claims to the visitor's attention between them, but from the purely visual point of view, the prettiest, and naturally the one with the green, is Ampney St Peter.

The old village pub is called 'The Packhorse', and this unspoiled little place has seen many travellers passing through over the centuries but has been content to go about its daily business without converting its quiet centre into a profitable tourist attraction.

Right across beyond the Cotswold edge near Stroud, Leonard Stanley — once called Stanley St Leonard to distinguish it from King's Stanley – has a green flanked by houses on one side and church on the other. The houses in this village are not all stone. Some are half-timbered, but the ones facing the church are stone-built. Can it have been here where John Wesley reckoned he drew a crowd of three thousand in 1735, when he preached 'in Stanley, on a little green near the town . . .'? He was, he wrote, 'strengthened to speak as I never did before, and continued speaking near two hours. The darkness of the night, and a little lightning, not lessening the number, but increasing the seriousness of the hearers.'

The village green is still a place of lawful assembly, but not even a speaker of Wesley's magnetism could hold a crowd of thirty, let alone three thousand, on a stormy night in these days of affluence and soap opera.

On the bank of the river below Gloucester, Frampton-on-Severn must be the last port of call in this section of our survey. Well out of the Cotswolds area of Gloucestershire now, we suddenly find here a very long and wide green of twenty acres, with half-timbered or Georgian brick houses, and the manor house and manor farm on opposite sides, all standing well back and giving the place a spacious air and a flatness we have hardly been used to lately. There is a duckpond toward the southern end and some thatch, too. Some say that the manor farm was the birthplace of 'Fair Rosamund', Henry II's mistress Rosamund Clifford, who was the object of Eleanor of Aquitaine's jealousy and of much medieval romance and ballad. The surviving stone parts of the present building with their mullioned windows do not date back farther than the fifteenth century, but who knows? There may be some truth in the tale.

——X——

The South West

AVON, SOMERSET, DEVON, CORNWALL, DORSET

As we progress towards the south-west corner of Britain, green villages peter out quite noticeably, and there is little in the new county of Avon to detain us in this context. Bathampton, near Bath, and Whitchurch, near Bristol, both support their Anglo-Saxon origins with little greens of no great significance, and we might notice in passing that the common at Frenchay, now enclosed by Bristol's suburbs, is where Dr W. G. Grace played some of his cricket; but we must pass on into Somerset to find anything worth a pause, and even in this villagey county such greens as there are must be carefully sought out.

One clue to the scarcity of greens is in the many double-barrelled village names. Cheddon Fitzpaine, Hardington Mandeville and Sampford Arundel are typical Somerset village names, and they denote, if not Norman origin of the settlements, at least Norman dominance and probably re-planning, so that the Anglo-Saxon village pattern has not commonly survived here.

Mells, near Frome, is an unusually stylish village of grey stone houses with fine church tower and manor house, with several small greens scattered about like confetti, and nearby is the hamlet of Mells Green, with stone cottages and a little stream making a peaceful traditional scene.

In and around the Mendip Hills, Priddy, Shipham and Loxton are among the original villages with a vestige of their former nuclei surviving. Priddy is a bleak and isolated former lead-mining village, and its three-acre green is a triangular one, which has been famous in the locality for its annual sheep fair. The church and former school stand higher up, on another, smaller green.

Shipham used to be a centre of calamine mining, where they brought up the zinc ore from which, among other things, the soothing lotion is made, and it is sobering to realize that the men and women whose centre of the social world was

island, Cornwall. A view
the quite large green at
e centre of this village
Bodmin Moor. Village
eens are extremely rare
Cornwall.

lpuddle, Dorset. A small
t historically important
een now preserved by
e National Trust.

kley, Surrey. A view
m the boundary –
cket on the long
egularly-shaped green
Ockley.

this acre of grass were miners and the wives of miners who spent their working lives underground obtaining this stuff that was necessary to the huge brass-foundries of Bristol.

Over to the east of Somerset, we leave all signs of industry, except agriculture, and find a village green at Wyke Champflower in spite of its Norman name – an acre and a half with plenty of trees round it, and close by is the manor house with the church attached to it, a very small Jacobean building with a battlemented bell turret and a fascinating interior.

High Ham, a remote village standing on high ground above the Somerset Levels near Langport, keeps its small green at the centre of what was once an island community in the medieval marshes. Such windswept spots as this cannot have seemed very hospitable to their residents through all the centuries before the attempts to drain the surrounding land. The Saxons called the local people the *'Seo-mere-saetan'* – 'the dwellers in the sea-lakes' – and from their description the county takes its name. But the people carried on here and maintained their little green on which to hold their village meetings and no doubt to provide their own entertainments, and in the fifteenth century they built themselves a fine church from the rock their hill is made of, with gargoyles that masons fashioned lovingly from the yielding stone.

Curry Rivel has a little oblong green of sorts, though there is nothing on it but the tension cable of an electricity pylon, so it hardly qualifies as one of the region's attractive greens, and we should move on hurriedly to East Coker, where we have not only a green but also one of the most delightful villages in Somerset. If you start from the foot of the hill by the stream, you can walk up past the rather formal-looking green, which seems to be an extension of the manor house garden on the other side of the wall. There are some fine ornamental trees on it. It is not clear what its legal status is. It may not be a village green in the strict sense at all; rather a concession to the villagers by a latter-day lord of the manor. However that may be, it is very attractive, and as you proceed past it up the slope, you come to a group of almshouses, built of stone with mullioned windows and gabled dormers, and beyond are the gates to the big house, Coker Court, and to the churchyard. All these buildings are of the mellow golden limestone from the quarries at Ham Hill, not far away.

This village was once preoccupied with making sailcloth, and it was the birthplace of a Puritan cordwainer, Andrew Eliot, who sailed to America in the seventeenth century and became Town Clerk of Boston, Massachusetts. A young descendant of his, Thomas, came to Britain in 1914 to study at Oxford, and stayed for the rest of his life, becoming a naturalized British subject. T. S. Eliot made East Coker the

inger, Surrey. Maypole
ncing is one of the
ditions at the annual
y fair on the green.

East Coker, Somerset. Pa[rt] of the walled green in th[e] stylish stone-built villag[e] associated with the poet T. S. Eliot.

subject of the second of his *Four Quarters* and asked that his ashes should be buried in the church, which in due course they were:

> Here, whence his forbears sprang, a man is
> laid
> As dust, in quiet earth . . .

Towards the western side of Somerset, a quartet of once-green villages in a line south from Taunton is worth noticing, at Trull, Corfe, Pitminster and Otterford. Here are names to conjure with. The greens at Pitminster and Otterford were of similar size, with the one at Trull tiny by comparison, and Corfe's only a small road-side green with a war memorial on it. Pitminster's former green, however, is a scruffy bit of waste land now being built on. Thus the quartet becomes a trio and will doubt-less be a duet soon. Trull, which has the M5 motorway roaring past it on one side and the spreading build-up of Taunton on the other, boasts a fine collection of medieval wood-carving in the church, where oak bench-ends show figures like those who knew this village when the church was being built – a peasant trudging along in ungainly boots, carrying a cross, and a man carrying a candle, for these are Christian pilgrims.

As we progress southward, we leave the Vale of Taunton and rise steadily into the Blackdown Hills, where the two-acre green at Otterford is on higher ground than the crossing of the River Otter which gave the place its name, a now scattered parish with a hilltop church.

The higher ground of west Somerset offers us another green village at Brompton Ralph – again the Norman name apparently hides Anglo-Saxon origins. This green is a small affair, in any case.

The villages nestling in the folds of Exmoor do not present much in our present context, but the green at Exford should not pass without notice. This high moorland village has undistinguished shops and houses round its fenced-in green, and several inns or hotels, for it was a well-known centre for stag-hunting once and is now a popular resort for touring the former royal forest. What you find happening on the central green depends when you go there. Sheep might be grazing it, or children playing on the swings at one end. There may be football or a cricket match, or just a man walking his dog, but whatever it is, there is visible evidence of this green's continuing importance for the local community's activities. Wrestling matches were held on it in the days when Blackmore set the story of Lorna Doone in the area, and John Fry noticed a crowd as he came into the village: '. . . as I coom down the hill. I zeed a saight of volks astapping of the ro-udway . . . "Wutt be up now?" I says to Bill the Blacksmith, "be the King acoomin?"'

The few villages of Devon which still have greens to show nearly all fall within that middle part of the county lying on what are called the Culm Measures – Carboniferous sandstone rocks and clay which support the mixed farming fields divided by lanes and tall banks and with deep river valleys cutting their way across the rolling landscape. Saxon infiltration into these parts was not so strong as elsewhere, so we should not *expect* to find too many villages with the central green nucleus. The Celtic pattern of scattered farmsteads is predominant here, as in the Welsh border country. Nevertheless, it is clear that there were once many more green villages in these parts than there are now. Look at a village such as Chittlehampton, where the finest village church tower in Devon stands above a square car-park with cottages round it, and you see a once-green village which has given up its green for the surfaced square which is very much in favour here – oddly enough, for this is usually an understandable inclination of industrial rather than rural villages. Little Torrington likewise has a car-parking area – unsurfaced at present – on what is whimsically signposted 'the village green'. Less obviously, Ashreigney has the

Exford, Somerset. Shops, houses and a hotel surround the green which is still at the centre of community life in this Exmoor village.

remains in front of its church of what was once a good-sized triangular green. A war memorial now stands on the surfaced area of the village centre with the general store and too many signs and cables all round.

Rose Ash has a small green with trees and seats near the church, but it cannot deceive anyone into thinking it was ever the communal centre of the settlement, any more than Beaford, where the rectangular green is enclosed by walls and hedges, with children's swings and such-like giving it the appearance of a playing field.

At Frithelstock, however, things look up a bit. There is a small triangular green here with a chestnut tree and a war memorial on it, but where the green ends and the lawn of the Clinton Arms begins is anybody's guess.

Bradworthy and Sutcombe, farther west, have both been credited with small greens, but Bradworthy is a classic example of the Devon nucleated village which now has a town-like square at its centre.

We should not expect to find cosy little green villages on the forbidding granite

ose Ash, Devon. A quiet
d attractive tree-shaded
een that does not look
e an ancient village
cleus, though the
urch is close by.

massif of Dartmoor, but at Mary Tavy on the west flank, and Manaton and North Bovey on the east, we do find village greens in this large and, from our present point of view, unfruitful county, where soon we may feel that the search is becoming desperate.

Mary Tavy is well known to industrial archaeologists, as old engine connoisseurs like to call themselves, for the best-preserved mine engine house in Devon, Wheal Betsy, and what was once the biggest copper mine in Europe. The old village had a substantial green until late in the nineteenth century, when the church underwent extensive and bad restoration, and at the same time the village lost most of its green which was incorporated into the churchyard.

North Bovey, however, on the opposite side of Dartmoor, still has a small green, heavily shaded by trees. The village hall stands on one side of the green, and the church is set back behind some cottages on the other. The village pump is preserved, and there is also a stone cross. The green was known as the 'playstow' once, when village children played in the shade of the oaks near their school building, long

since closed. The village pub is the Ring of Bells, and sitting here, almost uniquely in Devon, one can feel at the heart of a relatively unchanged village where the green is still the centre of all things. The village fair was imminent last time I was there, but how they accommodate it with all those trees in the way is beyond me.

The trees at Manaton, nearby, are plane trees and less overwhelming. They line the roadside of a long and vaguely triangular green, with the granite church tower of St Winifred rising above the thatched roofs of cottages on the other side. Manaton is an even quieter place than North Bovey, tucked away along moorland lanes, and its curiously secret green gives you a strange feeling that nothing has ever happened there. But it helps us to avoid writing off Devon completely as a source of green villages.

Cornwall, on the other hand, that very different land across the Tamar, could *almost* be written off without further ado, if it were not for the singular and most curious exception of Blisland, up on Bodmin Moor. What is this village doing with

eft: Frithelstock, Devon.
.he war memorial
roclaims this as a village
reen; otherwise it might
e mistaken for the front
.wn of the village pub.

elow: North Bovey,
evon. The 'playstow' is a
.llage green full of trees
ith the old pump and
one cross in their shade
nd the churchyard lych-
ate across the way.

a traditional green on the bleak Celtic peninsula where thin early settlement and subsequent industrial pollution have ensured that there is little sign of Anglo-Saxon origins left? The sloping green is a fairly large irregular one, with grey granite houses round it, and the church and Royal Oak inn on opposite sides. Blisland's church, dedicated to the Celtic Saints Proteus and Hyacinth, should not be missed by anyone who goes there. It is built of slate and granite and has a beautiful and interesting interior with granite columns that tilt alarmingly out of vertical. The late Sir John Betjeman called this 'the most beautiful of all the country churches of the West'.

Near the church is the former village school and library. There are plenty of seats on the green itself, and young trees have been planted to replace the big ones felled over the years – some of them elms lost in the recent epidemic. If it were not that too many wires and telegraph poles spoil the scene, this would be as good a green as can be found anywhere, which makes its uniqueness in Cornwall all the more remarkable.

It is not actually unique. It is just that no other green village in Cornwall gets mentioned in the guidebooks. There are greens at Lanivet, Polyphant, Trebullett and St Stephens-by-Launceston, among one or two other places, but they are small and insignificant.

We cannot leave this survey of England's village greens on such a negative note, and I have chosen to leave until last a look at Dorset. This delightful county is not any more notable for the number of its green villages than Devon or Cornwall, but it does have several features to bring a pleasant finale to our tour, as well as, by a strange freak, one of the most famous village greens in England.

First of all, Dorset brings a little revival of interest in those so-rural green names we became familiar with in the south-east. There are, for instance, Sleeping Green and Pamphill Green, the latter being a large common. And there is God's Blessing Green, near Wimborne Minster.

ft: Manaton, Devon.
*hatched cottages with
*anite walls separate
*urch from green in this
*iet Dartmoor village.

bove: Blisland, Cornwall.
*he Women's Institute
*bilee in 1965 occasioned
*e addition of this seat to
*ose already on the best
*f Cornwall's extremely
*re greens.

The stylish stone village of Nether Compton, near Sherborne, has a small green, though it is not the village nucleus, and Winterbourne Abbas, near Dorchester, also possesses a small green, though the place is a street village on the A35. The green at Winterborne St Martin down the road – otherwise known as Martinstown – is a famous fairground, not in the middle but at the east end of what is technically a street village, and it used to be the scene of horse- and sheep-dealing by gypsies who came from far and wide.

Up on Cranborne Chase, the highest village in Dorset is Ashmore, which has a sort of green centre almost entirely occupied by the village duckpond, about which are gathered various folk tales, such as the one that the pond used to attract gibbering creatures called Gappergennies. But that this large round pond intrudes on what was formerly a larger green seems to be indicated by the survival of a tradition called Filly-Loo, when villagers dance and sing round the pond at Midsummer, and Morris dancers join the festivities.

Tolpuddle's sloping green is at the centre of one of England's most famous historical events. Perhaps if there were any excuse for calling a green like, say, Benenden's in Kent, a 'conservative' green, Tolpuddle's would qualify without argument as a 'socialist' green. Here, in 1833, beneath the sycamore tree now propped up against collapse from old age, the six farmworkers met who became known as the Tolpuddle Martyrs. Their employers had agreed to wages of ten shillings a week, but cut them to nine shillings, then to eight, with further reductions threatened. George Loveless and his brother organized their fellow-workers into a union to protest at wages which made it 'impossible to live honestly'. They only broke the law when they took an oath of secrecy, and they were arrested and brought to trial at Dorchester for conspiracy.

There had been no threat of a strike, but the Nonconformist religion of the six alone branded them as dangerous radicals in the eyes of prosecution, jury and judge, and the latter sentenced them to seven years transportation. They were put in chains and shipped to Australia, while Robert Owen and others organized protests and petitions against the savagery of the sentence, with little effect until two years later, when Dr Thomas Wakley, a humanitarian and founder of the medical journal *The Lancet*, was instrumental in securing their pardon. By the time he got back to England, however, George Loveless had already served three years of his sentence, and some of his friends never came back. The connection of village greens with judicial savagery did not by any means end with the feudal system, and Tolpuddle's has become a place of pilgrimage for trade unionists everywhere. A group of cottages was put up by the TUC in 1934 as a permanent memorial to the martyrs, to be occupied by elderly farmworkers.

Tolpuddle is in no sense a 'green' village. It lies along the busy A35 between Dorchester and Bournemouth. But its little quarter-acre of green, with the Martyrs' Tree on it now protected by the National Trust, stands as a symbol of this Anglo-Saxon type of communal centre which we have traced throughout England, and it seems a highly appropriate if diminutive green at which to end our exploration.

The Future of Village Greens

It would require a supreme optimist to deny that village greens are on the way to oblivion, no matter how slow that process may be. The pressures of modern population and traffic, combined with the relative uselessness of most of the small village greens today, must undoubtedly mean that they will gradually be done away with.

There is no immediate danger to most of the larger greens, which still serve as fair or cricket grounds or are legally subject to common rights. And even the smaller greens are safe enough if they have some value as tourist attractions. The greens most in danger are the smaller ones which have no further use for the community, particularly in places like the industrial Midlands. Cricket may have been played on such greens once, but sponsorship has now shifted the game to a larger and flatter field where budding Bothams can exercise their skills without the unpredictable intervention of cowpats and duckponds. Dancing round the maypole has long been given up as old-fashioned in such materialistic places, and the church fête once held annually on the green now takes place on the vicarage lawn. So the green now stands, supporting nothing but a signpost and a bus stop, at the centre of an increasingly busy commuter village where young executives negotiate their polished cars each morning round an area which would, they assert, be much better as a surfaced square with a traffic island and a concrete lamp-post in the middle.

They and other like-minded capitalist folk who see village greens as so much waste land would have got short shrift from William Cobbett, who saw that no rural open space was 'waste' if it afforded fresh air and exercise to youngsters who might otherwise be hanging around filthy city streets.

I am not among those who maintain fanatically that everything old must be preserved at all cost. The English village is a permanently changing and living thing,

and it should not be rendered static so that it becomes a museum instead of a rural community, as one or two famous tourist villages have almost become in recent years. The charm of our English villages is not that they look as they did two hundred or five hundred years ago – for none of them do – but that they represent at one and the same time both the conservative tradition and the tradition of dissent in England. They stay stubbornly behind the times by the standards of the towns and cities and support the conservative temperament of the English by holding back from the headlong rush of industrial man towards a uniform and faceless civilization: more practical and efficient, maybe, but impulsive, mechanical and heartless.

So changes to our village scene should not, and indeed cannot, be stopped, but they ought to be watched closely and monitored. Once you have made the mistake of inflicting the death penalty on an important feature of a village, it cannot be resurrected, and the village green, whatever its original purpose may have been,

ft: Hillam, North
orkshire. A one-time
mmunal green reduced
ludicrous proportions
the demands of modern
affic.

remains one of the most ancient and characteristic symbols of our Englishness, like a green coverlet in the cradle of infant Anglia.

I think the time may be approaching when some of our best village greens will require strict preservation orders to be made, in order to prevent building encroachment, despoliation by too many signs, cables and litter-bins, and other misuses. It is no use waiting until it is too late. Some modest protection against enclosure was given to greens in the 1845 General Inclosure Act, but that did not prevent the disappearance of many greens since that time, and even since the reinforced protection of the 1925 Law of Property Act some greens have been encroached upon or removed wholesale, presumably on the highly debatable principle that the change was for the 'benefit of the neighbourhood'. The consuming advance of the industrial mentality into our rural communities goes on almost unobserved. Once there were untold thousands of village greens throughout England. Now there are perhaps hardly more than fifteen hundred.

ght: Chittlehampton,
evon. This village
uare, characteristic of
e south-west, may have
en a green once, or if
ot, it served the same
urpose. Now it is a
r-park.

Today, the final arbiter of what may and may not be done with village greens is the Department of the Environment (subject, of course, to the law of the land). I have said that all village greens are the common property of the villagers. In a few cases, the land which includes the village green is still in the ownership of the 'lord of the manor', but the owner is bound by law to recognize the rights of the villagers on the green, which include the right to play games and so on. Where

low: Snowshill,
oucestershire. The
urchyard gradually
ok over the green at the
ntre of this Cotswold
lage.

parish councils administer greens on behalf of the community, they can make by-laws which are, in theory, supposed to protect the villagers' interests but do not always do so.

We have noticed in this book former greens which have been taken over as churchyards or school playgrounds, converted into surfaced car-parks or reduced to shapeless and useless fragments by new roads cutting through them. Here a local council may have granted permission for a hideous concrete bus shelter with a corrugated iron roof to be built on the edge of a green; and there a local businessman

got permission to extend his garage onto the green by a foot or two. Gradually the rights of village Englishmen are pared away, and by the time we all come to our senses and realize that these greens were the things we loved most about our country villages and hamlets, it will be too late. You can lay out a new green, but it will not be the same as the old one, with its historical associations and local traditions and collective memories going back over a thousand years, with that community sense of a direct link with the Anglo-Saxon settlers who founded the village after the Romans left Britain. The old men of the village will not sit under the ancient oak shaking their heads over the backward defensive strokes of the local lad who now plays for the county, or the rum folk who have come to live in the village. They will be strangers there themselves, and the village continuity broken as certainly as if it were Goldsmith's deserted village:

> Dear lovely bowers of innocence and ease,
> Seats of my youth, when every sport could please,
> How often have I loitered o'er thy green,
> Where humble happiness endeared each scene!
> How often have I paused on every charm,
> The sheltered cot, the cultivated farm,
> The never-failing brook, the busy mill,
> The decent church that topped the neighbouring hill,
> The hawthorn bush, with seats beneath the shade,
> For talking age and whispering lovers made!

Is this just sentimental claptrap? If the nature of our civilization is changing, why not just let the rural scene follow in the wake of the urban landscape without trying to control it by legislation? If village greens do eventually disappear, so what? They have served their purpose and are no longer necessary; future generations will not miss them if they are not there.

This kind of argument often has much reason in its favour, and generally speaking, it is a philosophy I tend towards myself if we are discussing torn-up hedgerows or derelict buildings. In the one case, the first priority of our farmers is to produce the nation's food, and if efficient machinery demands bigger fields, so be it. The small fields we want to preserve for ever are hardly more than two hundred years old, anyway. The countryside has changed before, and it can change again. In the other case, many people seem to me zealously over-protective about useless old buildings which are often ugly as well. We should be much less anxious as a nation about *things* and much more concerned about *people*.

I take a different view about village greens precisely because they *are* about people, although we may have difficulty in recognizing the fact today. Greens are bound

208

up with the English character in a way that buildings can never be, for they are always temporary things; even if 'temporary' means four hundred years, it is a short time compared with the life of a village green. We have learned our community strengths and weaknesses not shut up in our individual homes in isolation but out there on the communal greens among our fellow men. We have, as it were, cut our teeth on them. They are the pivots round which our Englishness revolves. The common Englishman felt a sense of belonging there, I dare say, when the Christian church seemed nothing more than a place for ritual intonement in a language he did not understand.

We have developed our sense of humour there over more than a thousand years, and learned to face adversity with that community morale which has served us well through two world wars in the present century. And young lovers have shared the shade of the common oak when there was nowhere else for them to lie, and perhaps conceived great men beneath the stars at night:

> There is a small green place
>   Where cowslips early curled,
> Which on sabbath day I trace,
>   The dearest in the world.
> A little oak spreads o'er it,
>   And throws a shadow round,
> A green sward close before it,
>   The greenest ever found:
> There is not a woodland nigh nor is there a green grove,
> Yet stood the fair maid nigh me and told me all her love.
>
> (John Clare)

Before the Industrial Revolution the vast majority of Englishmen lived in villages, earning their living from the land and satisfied to spend their lives among the communities they were born into. If that kind of lifestyle has formed the English nation over a period of well over a thousand years, how can we be so confident, after a little more than a century, that we have forsaken these roots forever and shall never yearn for them again?

When we look seriously at that time-scale, it seems that we have become a technological nation almost impulsively, as a child is fascinated by a new toy. We may yet long for the faithful old teddy bear we grew up with, for all our self-exaltation as the beneficiaries of a modern capitalist society.

In his futuristic novel *Seven Days in New Crete*, in which men have been forced to turn the clock back as the only alternative to extinction, Robert Graves postulates a village called Rabnon where a council of war is held on the village green, following

the disclosure that boys from the neighbouring village are being fed nothing but damson jam for their suppers. With the villagers 'squatting in a semi-circle in front of the totem pole' and the elders 'seated on rush-bottomed chairs at the back', the situation is discussed and someone recalls that the two villages once went to war for less provocation than this – over a howling dog. War is declared, to be fought on the following Tuesday ('We always fight our wars on Tuesdays'). The rival armies are drawn up on opposite sides of the boundary between the two villages. The men are half naked and well greased. Rabnon's objective is to carry a bunch of painted wooden damsons over the opposing village's green and force it into the mouth of a godling at the base of their totem pole. The war is reminiscent of Shrovetide football matches and the Easter bottle-kicking game at Hallaton, Leicestershire. The worst casualties are a broken collarbone and a sprained ankle, and a feast is held when it is all over. 'Only neighbours know each other well enough to go to war,' says

210

rcebridge, Durham.
e modern village is on
e site of a large Roman
t. Its fine rectangular
een has been the heart
the English settlement
perhaps a thousand
ars.

one of Graves's characters. Would that our absurd territorial rivalries could be so wisely contained today.

However, the memorials we have erected to the dead of two world wars have dignified small bits of land that were hardly more than roadside waste before, and given them a status, as places of community pride and purpose. Legally and morally, if not historically, these grass patches deserve the same recognition and preservation as village greens, and in most cases they get it. But *all* village greens, whether they have war memorials on them or not, are monuments to the men and women who have lived and died during fifteen hundred years to make the communities what they are today, and it is short-sighted of those villages which have allowed their ancient greens to decline into litter-covered and untended grassland fit only for supporting signposts or bus stops where once maypoles or market crosses stood as the focal points of community life. The signpost and the bus stop are symbols only of the modern age's restlessness – the green is no longer a centre or nucleus but merely a departure point on the way to somewhere else.

You could take almost any Englishman and sit him down on a village green on a summer's day, shaded from the sun by native trees with birds twittering in their branches, with a medieval church over in one corner and a cosy-looking oak-beamed pub in another, and say, 'This is the *real* England.' And he would believe you, whether he came from the steelworks or the oil rig, from the middle of London or the sidings at Crewe. There are very few things that all Englishmen would agree about so easily. So let us keep a careful watch over our greens, realizing that what is claimed for Meriden is in a real sense true of every village green throughout the land – it is the very heart of England.

APPENDIX:

The Top Twenty Village Greens of England

This list is a purely personal one, of course, and just for fun. But if all the village greens of England were to be swept away by government dictate (anything is possible), leaving just twenty to be preserved as outstanding conservation areas, these are the twenty I would probably vote for, all things considered. They are in alphabetical order.

Aldbury, Hertfordshire   A classic green of the Home Counties type, surrounded by vernacular building in brick and timber and complete with duckpond. It has made several appearances in films and on television in one guise or another.

Bearsted, Kent   This square and beautiful six-acre green is chiefly famous today for its cricket associations – Alfred Mynn played on it, among other great cricketers – but it is also important historically as the place where Wat Tyler gathered his followers for their abortive Peasants' Revolt. Though the village is now practically a suburb of Maidstone, its green is a precious piece of old rural England.

Bishop Burton, Humberside   Chestnut trees, pond, village pump and war memorial grace this well-kept green where ducks and geese congregate noisily. The green is surrounded by pantiled cottages and stone walls and is among the most idyllic of English greens.

Cavendish, Suffolk   The most picturesque of East Anglian greens, it is one of the three or four most-photographed village greens in England and has appeared on calendars and chocolate boxes galore. The church tower and thatched cottages help to make the picture, so they need to be preserved too.

East Witton, North Yorkshire   An ancient village green of outstanding historical and social value, as it seems to form a link between the Anglo-Saxon pattern of settlement in England and the feudal *solskifte* system of northern Europe. Although the village has been rebuilt more than once by lords of the manor, it almost certainly retains its original layout.

Evenley, Northamptonshire   One of the best of the Midland greens, with attractive limestone cottages neatly arranged round its four equal sides. It has some fine trees offering welcome shade round its perimeter on hot summer days, from which to watch the cricket being played in the middle.

213

Finchingfield, Essex Certainly one of the most photogenic of all village greens, it also has the classic features of the Anglo-Saxon village nucleus – triangular shape, church, village inn and pond, with houses grouped cosily and informally round it.

Haddenham, Buckinghamshire A very attractive and completely rustic green with a duckpond right up against the wall of the churchyard and interesting thatched houses and farm buildings round its irregular shape. A green that looks as if it has remained the same for centuries.

Hartley Wintney, Hampshire Cricketers Green is one of the finest village greens on which cricket is still played, with a splendid timber pavilion and the Cricketers Inn alongside, and of a size where you really have to hit the ball to reach the boundary. Yet it is a traditional green with pleasant houses round it.

Long Melford, Suffolk The sheer stylishness of this long, triangular green entitles it to its place here. The village school is at the foot of the gentle slope upwards to the magnificent parish church, with in between them Melford Hall, the Trinity Hospital almshouses and other fine buildings, mostly of mellow brick.

Lower Slaughter, Gloucestershire This village green is undeniably 'picturesque' in the sense that it works like a magnet on tourists with cameras, but seen in the winter, when the village is left to its quiet self, it has a charm which surely qualifies it for inclusion among the best village greens of England.

Marsh Baldon, Oxfordshire This is an extremely large green, unusual in southern England, with houses surrounding what was formerly a square shape. It is a most interesting green, legally and historically. Rights to its use have been much fought over, as gates have been used to deny public access at certain times.

Milburn, Cumbria This large, rectangular green must be preserved as being of outstanding interest for social history. It is the classic example of the village green seen as a piece of defensive strategy. Completely surrounded by vernacular building in rugged northern stone, and with the village school and a maypole standing on it, as well as grazing livestock.

Nun Monkton, North Yorkshire I have included this green as an excellent example of the long but irregularly shaped greens characteristic of Yorkshire, though this one is vaguely triangular. It has a horse-pond and a maypole, with brick-built cottages round it and an avenue leading off to the village church.

Piercebridge, Durham The best example of the very long, rectangular green familiar in Durham, completely surrounded by good houses and attractively laid out with trees. It might be hard to picture in this heavily industrialized county today, but this green was meant for sheep and cattle.

Selborne, Hampshire It is only small, but world famous, and must be counted among the 'untouchables' on account of its association with the naturalist-parson Gilbert White, whose home and church were beside it and who knew it intimately. It is called 'The Plestor' and is already safe in the hands of the National Trust.

Tissington, Derbyshire   This is one of the best examples of what we might call the 'model' green – created, nurtured and preserved by the Fitzherbert lords of the manor. It is a triangular green enhanced by exquisite buildings in the pale local limestone.

Tolpuddle, Dorset   It is hardly one of the most spectacular greens in England, but highly significant as a place which, even in the nineteenth century, served its purpose as a communal meeting place where working people discussed their grievances against their employers, as peasants had done under the feudal system a thousand years before.

Urchfont, Wiltshire   Although it is dominated by a large duckpond, this green is at the centre of a beautiful and stylish village which ought not to be interfered with in the slightest degree. Fine brick houses stand behind golden conifers and spreading cedars which shade the happy ducks from the sun.

Wisborough Green, West Sussex   I have chosen this as the best of the large irregular greens of southern England. Its houses are sited with casual informality round its tree-lined edges in company with the village pub, church and shops. The original green may well have been the triangular bit where the church is.

Sources

In addition to the large number of topographical works and guidebooks I have consulted during the course of this work, to all of which I am indebted, I must mention the following more specialized works which I have found most helpful.

MAURICE BERESFORD & JOHN G. HURST (Eds.), *Deserted Medieval Villages*, Lutterworth Press, 1971

R. W. BRUNSKILL, *Vernacular Architecture of the Lake Counties*, Faber, 1974

JOHN BURKE, *The English Inn*, Batsford, 1981

JOHN CLARE, *Selected Poems*, Everyman's Library, 1965

WILLIAM COBBETT, *Rural Rides*, Everyman's Library edition, 1973

H. C. DARBY (Ed.), *A New Historical Geography of England before 1600*, Cambridge University Press, 1976

GILLIAN DARLEY, *Villages of Vision*, Architectural Press, 1975

DANIEL DEFOE, *A Tour Through the Whole Island of Great Britain*, Penguin edition, 1971

GEORGE EWART EVANS, *The Pattern under the Plough*, Faber, 1966

GEORGE FOX, *Journal*, Everyman's Library edition, 1949

J. G. FRAZER, *The Golden Bough*, Macmillan, 1978 edition

G. N. GARMONSWAY (Tr.), *The Anglo-Saxon Chronicle*, Everyman's Library edition, 1972

ROBERT GRAVES, *Seven Days in New Crete*, Cassell, 1949

PAUL HAIR (Ed.), *Before the Bawdy Court*, Elek, 1972

W. G. HOSKINS, *The Making of the English Landscape*, Hodder & Stoughton, 1955

W. G. HOSKINS & L. DUDLEY STAMP, *The Common Lands of England and Wales*, Collins, 1963

A. G. MACDONELL, *England their England*, Macmillan, 1933

RICHARD MUIR, *The Lost Villages of Britain*, Michael Joseph, 1982

N. PEVSNER AND OTHERS, *The Buildings of England*, Penguin Books, 46 vols., 1951–74

TREVOR ROWLEY, *Villages in the Landscape*, Dent, 1978

C. T. SMITH, *An Historical Geography of Western Europe before 1800*, Longmans Green, 1967

PHILIP ZIEGLER, *The Black Death*, Collins, 1969

Index

Note: Place names with prefixes such as East Dean and Great Tew are indexed by the prefix.